Olivier Urbain is Director of the Toda In:
Policy Research and the Founder and Director
Network. He was formerly Professor of Modern
at Soka University, Japan, and is the Founder o   ... . and
Peace of the International Peace Research Association. Publications include
numerous articles about the power of the arts for peace, and the book *Daisaku
Ikeda's Philosophy of Peace* (2010). He edited *Music and Conflict Transformation*
(2008) and co-edited *Music and Solidarity* (2011).

Dialogue is our most vital and enduring means of resolving conflicts and
engendering mutual understanding. SGI President Daisaku Ikeda has been a
globally prominent practitioner and enabler of dialogue for several decades. He
has participated in dialogues with world leaders, Nobel laureates, peace and
rights activists, and grass-roots citizens, ubiquitously and tirelessly furthering
the cause of world peace by cultivating global humanism.

In this important anthology – *Daisaku Ikeda and Dialogue for Peace* – editor
Olivier Urbain convenes a stellar assembly of Ikeda scholars and accomplished
dialogicians, who address salient dimensions of Mr. Ikeda's philosophy of
dialogue, and of peace. Their insightful essays are must-reads for anyone
interested in the role of dialogue in diplomacy, Buddhism, education, and
crisis management. This book is a string of pearls for peace, an invaluable gift
to our global village in the twenty-first century, and beyond.

> – **Lou Marinoff**, Ph.D., Professor of Philosophy,
> The City College of New York, co-author with Daisaku Ikeda of
> *The Inner Philosopher: Conversations on Philosophy's Transformative Power.*

Olivier Urbain has captured some of the key issues in this book from the
writings and speeches of Daisaku Ikeda. Apart from the fact that Mr. Ikeda
has personal experience of the hardships of life under repression, he has
developed an originality of thought from dialogue with great thinkers of our
times. This is so very important for our present times. As we go through the
many apprehensive experiences of life in this century, we begin to realize the
importance of indigenous knowledge systems and of learning to think out
of the box. Over the years we have been conditioned to a discourse that we
have accepted to be the final truth and yet there are people like Mr. Ikeda
who clearly indicate that there is another way, another system of thought
that is not only powerful but also has the tremendous potential to lead
our world into peace and contentment. Gandhi once said, "True morality
consists not in following the beaten track, but in finding out the true path
for ourselves and in fearlessly following it." Mr. Ikeda's words and ideas are

innovative and need to be studied and applied. This book will therefore be of tremendous value.

– **Ela Gandhi**, Social activist, granddaughter of
Mahatma Gandhi, former Chancellor of the Durban University of
Technology and former Member of Parliament, South Africa.

Daisaku Ikeda and Dialogue for Peace is a timely companion to the earlier publication of *Daisaku Ikeda's Philosophy of Peace* in 2010 by Olivier Urbain that expands our understanding about Ikeda's views on peace through a set of articles that examine the philosophy and praxis of *dialogue* – the central means with which Ikeda believes that peace is achieved. Whether it be in attaining inner transformation or sound political negotiations, in realizing our interconnectedness with others or collective identity as global citizens, in exploring our distinct differences or individual personal histories – *dialogue* is the educational medium through which individuals can consciously transform their existential conditions into cultures of peace in this forthcoming century. The importance of this collective volume is that it brings Ikeda's works into closer dialogue with traditional academic discourse in fields of education, politics, philosophy, and culture; something that is essential to further strengthen the formal impact of peace education in academia and informally on a global scale. I recommend this volume in tandem with Urbain's previous book for those approaching their studies of peace leaders from a transdisciplinary perspective and seeking excellent references on Ikeda's philosophy of peace.

– **B. Jeannie Lum**, Ph.D., Associate Professor,
Department of Educational Foundations,
University of Hawai'i at Manoa. Editor,
Journal of Peace Education.

Olivier Urbain, in writing *Daisaku Ikeda's Philosophy of Peace* (2010), made a major contribution to the development of societies globally, by providing an academic work in which the powerful values and principles articulated by Ikeda could be understood better and shared widely. I welcome this new book on Ikeda's philosophy of "dialogue for peace," which contains chapters written by members of a growing worldwide network of academics. Parts 2 and 3 are especially relevant in Northern Ireland where there is a real need to realize that dialogue at its best is not about having the skills to win arguments, but is rather about our capacity to connect based on our common humanity, about having, as Ikeda mentioned in his famous speech at Columbia University in 1996, the "compassion to maintain an imaginative empathy that reaches beyond our immediate surroundings."

The philosophy and practices of Ikeda need to be included – and more widely discussed – in the peace studies literature, and on conference agendas. They should also be more accessible to students, particularly in Higher Education. To facilitate this process, it is vital that this book reaches as many people as possible, enhancing the development of a culture of peace. As mentioned in the preface by Stuart Rees, Ikeda wrote: "It is crucial to revive the spirit of dialogue and to unleash a creative search for peaceful co-existence. To have faith in the promise of dialogue is to believe in the promise of humanity." This must happen in this century.

– **Pauline Murphy**, Ph.D., Emerita Professor,
Social Inclusion, University of Ulster, Belfast.

In this volume, Olivier Urbain has collected chapters which illustrate the next generation of thinking about the contributions of dialogue to the multi-level peace process and the prevention of future conflict. As we strive for global citizenship and a common humanity, there are increasing demands on each of us to take part in the practice of peacemaking through dialogue. Reflecting on Ikeda's work, Urbain emphasizes that dialogue is a practical process: looking for common ground and, at the same time, respectfully recognizing differences.

– **Linda M. Johnston**, Ph.D., President,
International Peace Research Association Foundation.

In *Daisaku Ikeda and Dialogue for Peace*, editor Olivier Urbain and all the contributors advance a powerful international and intergenerational dialogue on peace and justice. That ongoing conversation has huge reach over space and time, and also over modes of thought. It provides a model for the kind of probing dialogue that Daisaku Ikeda has advocated for decades. Is there another book that so sensibly begins with the Lotus Sutra and ends with ways to abolish nuclear weapons? This dialogue is a gift to all who seek a future of peace and justice in the world.

– **George Kent**, Ph.D., Professor of Political Science (Emeritus),
University of Hawai'i at Manoa.

In a world facing severe environmental, social, political and spiritual crises, in large part due to poor engagement and communication between peoples, this work offers us precious insights inspired by the thoughts and work of Daisaku Ikeda. Olivier Urbain and his collaborators thoughtfully reflect on Ikeda's principles of dialogue and thereby demonstrate how a global culture of peace could be fostered which could transform our world in profoundly positive ways. This book is a must-read for anyone committed to fostering a better world.

– **Freya Higgins-Desbiolles**, Ph.D., Senior Lecturer,
Department of Tourism, University of Otago.

This volume is very timely as we engage in new global socio-economic relations and environmental conflicts. It reclaims dialogue for peace as "strategic" humanitarianism: our tool kit to enable human and environmental security through global citizenship. Dialogue for peace is given scant regard in a world preoccupied with "strategic" militarism. The patriarchal home; complacent civil society; authoritarian boardroom; greedy global market place; and divisive international political arena, are all examples. Yet, dialogue for peace is precisely what we need in all these locations.

As courageous peace with justice advocate Aung San Suu Kyi has said "We have to choose between dialogue or utter devastation." Such instruction for global citizenship is grounded in a spirit of Buddhism – as elaborated in the writings and demonstrated in the actions of Daisaku Ikeda.

– **Lynda-ann Blanchard**, Ph.D., Professor,
Centre for Human Rights Education; and Centre for Peace and
Conflict Studies, University of Sydney, Australia.

DAISAKU IKEDA AND DIALOGUE FOR PEACE

Edited by

Olivier Urbain

in association with
The Toda Institute for Global Peace and Policy Research

Published in 2013 by I.B.Tauris & Co Ltd
6 Salem Road, London W2 4BU
175 Fifth Avenue, New York NY 10010
www.ibtauris.com

Distributed in the United States and Canada Exclusively by Palgrave Macmillan
175 Fifth Avenue, New York NY 10010

Toda Institute book series on Global Peace and Policy

ISBN: 978 1 78076 572 3 (pb)
ISBN: 978 1 78076 571 6 (hb)

A full CIP record for this book is available from the British Library
A full CIP record is available from the Library of Congress

Library of Congress Catalog Card Number: available

Typeset in Garamond by Initial Typesetting Services, Edinburgh
Printed and bound in Great Britain by T.J. International, Padstow, Cornwall

Contents

Notes on Contributors

Christine Atieno is the Chairperson and Co-founder of South–South Network Engagement – Africa, a Founding Core Group of the South–South Network International Secretariat and a member of the International Peace Research Association. She is a Peace-Building consultant who has worked and made progressive achievements for regional and international organizations namely Feminenza International, Kenya Chapter Representative – Finance (2007–2008); South Sudan Peace Commission/ Sudan Peace and Reconciliation Commission/ Convergent International, Program Officer (2004–2006) and Geneva Call, Program Assistant (2000–2003).

Elizabeth Bowen is the former Director of the Peace, Culture and Education department of SGI Australia and an independent researcher. She has a doctorate in Social Policy and Welfare, having focused her research on young people, changes in employment and risk. In collaboration, Elizabeth Bowen has contributed to an exhibition and seminars on depression, titled *Dark to Dawn: Being Creative about Depression*.

Jason Goulah is Associate Professor and Director of Bilingual-Bicultural Education and Director of World Languages Education at DePaul University in Chicago, Illinois, USA. His research interests include transformative learning approaches to second and world language education; Makiguchi and Ikeda studies in education and language, culture, identity and multiple literacies. His scholarship on Daisaku Ikeda has appeared in the *Peace Studies Journal* and numerous other academic journals and edited volumes.

Wayne Hudson is Professor of Humanities in the School of Philosophy at the University of Tasmania and Strategic Research Professor at Charles Sturt University, Canberra. He has published more than 25 books and is interested in how the emerging global civilization can learn from movements such as Soka Gakkai International.

Yoichi Kawada is the director of the Institute of Oriental Philosophy (IOP). He received a Ph.D. in immunology in 1968 and is a recognized authority in Buddhist history and philosophy, bringing the insights of Buddhism to bear on contemporary issues of bioethics, medical and clinical practice.

Kimiaki Kawai is Program Director of Peace Affairs at Soka Gakkai International (SGI) and Director of the Soka Gakkai Peace Committee. He is a graduate of Tokyo University of Foreign Studies and has been engaged in work on a variety of peace activities.

Gonzalo Obelleiro is a doctoral student of philosophy and education at Teachers College, Columbia University, and a graduate of Soka University of America. He was born and raised in Argentina. His current work focuses on cosmopolitanism, value creation, and the educational philosophy of Daisaku Ikeda. He is the first recipient of Soka University of America's highest academic award, the Founders Award, and a former Education Fellow at the Ikeda Center for Peace, Learning, and Dialogue.

Stuart Rees is Professor Emeritus at the Center for Peace and Conflict Studies at the University of Sydney, Australia and Chair of the Sydney Peace Foundation. In 2005 he was awarded the Order of Australia for services to international relations.

Hirotomo Teranishi is Director of the International Institute for Advanced Buddhology (IRIAB) in Tokyo. He is also Professor of the Faculty of Economics and Vice-President of Soka University in Tokyo, Japan.

Olivier Urbain is Director of the Toda Institute for Global Peace and Policy Research and the Founder and Director of the Transcend: Art & Peace Network. He was formerly Professor of Modern Languages and Peace Studies at Soka University, Japan, and is the Founder of the Commission on Art and Peace of the International Peace Research Association. Publications include numerous articles about the power of the arts for peace, and the book *Daisaku Ikeda's Philosophy of Peace* (2010). He edited *Music and Conflict Transformation* (2008) and co-edited *Music and Solidarity* (2011).

Preface

Breaking Boundaries and Challenging Conventional Wisdom through Dialogue

Stuart Rees

Daisaku Ikeda's contribution to human well-being derives from his challenges to conventions and from his refusal to be controlled by religious, political or cultural orthodoxy. That claim can be illustrated by his commitment to dialogue, fully expressed in his leadership of the Soka Gakkai, his meaningful dialogues with world leaders and his inspiration of young people. Yet in respect to these achievements there remains a mystery: what sort of person risks challenges and change; what sort of individual resists authority, particularly in a culture which encourages conformity?

Biographical clues

One answer to this question derives from a portrayal of a leader who inspires, who shows impressive stamina and who knows how to evaluate his goals and the means of achieving them. Ikeda's vision, argues Olivier Urbain (2010, 22), derives from those character-forming experiences of war, the death of his eldest brother and the influence of his great mentor Josei Toda. That leader's humility, courage and belief in the potential of all human beings to realize the qualities of a common humanity greatly influenced the young Ikeda. Yet Ikeda's personal losses and the plight of a defeated Japan might have produced an opposite reaction – a desire for revenge or a sense of fatalism that nothing could be done because huge outside influences, such as Japanese humiliation and US occupation, would stifle any individual initiative.

Why did he not settle for a life of conformity that could have given rewards and would never have required any passion for peace? Instead, however, he became a young man with a sense of urgency about injustice learning from Toda about the responsibility to serve humanity and about a Buddhist vision of a joy for life and a love of all living things.

The notion "all living things" highlights Ikeda's belief in people's inter-dependence and from this belief came his commitment to education for global citizenship. An Australian metaphor refers to a need in politics and in each individual's life time journey to search for a light on the hill. The Buddhist ideal of the bodhisattva – the person who strives without cease for the happi-ness of others – appears to be Ikeda's light on the hill.

The vision which Ikeda has passed on to millions came from Toda, from a cosmopolitan interpretation of Buddhism and from a commitment to the welfare of others, in particular through a striving to achieve world peace. Those influences can be identified, but how were they translated into action? A first response to this question concerns the stamina of an individual who felt that there were seldom enough hours in the day to realize his goals. An impression of unusual stamina comes from the 20 years in which Ikeda was engaged in writing *The Human Revolution*. He explained. "I utilized every spare moment I could find to push forward with my narrative, page by page" (Ikeda 2004a, viii).

Of inner transformation

The means of recharging one's physical and spiritual batteries usually provide the stamina required to confront uphill struggles. In Ikeda's case, the process of inner transformation appears to be that means. Although I'm a trifle skeptical of a "great man" theory of history – the idea that the course of events can be explained by the actions of significant individuals – nevertheless Ikeda's lessons about the value of inner transformation do explain the link between his personal agendas and his diverse political, literary and organizational achievements.

Inner transformation is a far more complex process than what the American corporate world calls "self-improvement." Urbain defines inner transformation as "the personal efforts of individuals to enhance their own courage, wisdom and compassion through any spiritual or philosophical tradition or means available" (Urbain 2010, 109). From such transformation comes the energy and courage to strive for peace. Yet the quality of courage is not inherent; nor is it the product of a momentary whim. A striving for global citizenship and for world peace imposes daily demands, involves risks and takes practice. The experience of taking risks can be part of transformation and may simultaneously confront those questions of identity: who are you, what do you stand for? Reminders about the significance of courage and compassion would come from such reflection, but that still does not explain the cosmopolitan nature of Ikeda's work: his outlook remained global when he could have stayed local. To explain such international perspectives, we need to consider his commitment to dialogue.

Significance of dialogue

President Ikeda is a fascinating person to meet. His welcomes are warm and his observations spontaneous. In discussions about the possible links between an individual's biography and their work for peace, he peppers conversations with touches of self-deprecation and other humor. A mundane interpretation of this commitment to dialogue is that it makes life more interesting, avoids self-centeredness – let alone any preoccupation with the alleged merits of one's own country and culture. But there's a lot more to Ikeda's conduct of dialogue than that. In the interests of peace, dialogue is a way to demystify stereotypes, to question the claims of experts, to find humanity in the people who might have been seen as enemies. Politically astute exchanges explain the internationalism of Ikeda and of the Soka Gakkai International (SGI). They also display his challenges to authority.

Such challenges occurred against a background of Japanese militarism, nationalism and imperialism. His encouragement to others not to be co-opted by authority is also surprising in the context of those 50 years since the end of World War II which saw the flourishing of a highly controlling and influential Japanese corporatism.

Ikeda contrasts the ideals of Buddhism with diverse abuses of authority:

> The value of Buddhism
> lies in its elucidation
> of principles for living.
> The evil nature of authority
> lies in its malicious distortions
> and destructive intent (Ikeda 2004b, 69).

He also pleads,

> Never believe
> that the greatest
> most irresistible force
> is the power of the state.

A few paradoxes

My appraisal of such a humanist leader merits a pause. I want to consider how the chemistry of Ikeda's personal characteristics led him to be so creative in administrative and artistic terms. The creativity appears to emerge from several paradoxes: a disdain for authority yet he is a significant authority figure, a commitment to Buddhism yet he is fiercely secular in advocating respect for others' beliefs and interests, a significant Japanese citizen yet an obvious internationalist. Regarding the latter he observes,

> In Einstein's impassioned cry:
> We must try to awaken in people
> a sense of solidarity that will not stop
> at national borders (Ikeda 2004b, 112).

In the long poem *In Joyous Tumult*, he confronts questions of authority:

> In the words
> of a wise child –
> Discard the symbols

of authority you have
so proudly pinned
to your chest (Ikeda 2004b, 52).

He inspires others yet also prompts deference. He advocates equality:

Here there is no
class struggle.
Ours is a humanism
in which all are equal (Ikeda 2004b, 53).

Yet Ikeda is the highly significant head of an organization whose effectiveness appears to depend in part on the maintenance of hierarchies of power. He has dedicated his life to a common humanity yet his followers often appear cautious about taking explicit stands on pressing human rights issues – the plight of the Palestinians or regarding the current controversy over freedom of expression as illustrated by US politicians' claims that Julian Assange, a co-founder of Wikileaks, is a terrorist and should be assassinated.

Ikeda's inspiration from Buddhism has contributed to a secular value-based education system which also acknowledges international influences, as in the respect paid to such figures as Albert Einstein, Victor Hugo, Michel de Montaigne and the iconoclastic American poet Walt Whitman. Ikeda's curiosity and his stress on inclusiveness produces the telling paradox of an emphasis on spirituality tinged with secularism, a deep respect for individual belief coupled to a striving for global citizenship.

These apparent contradictions emerge from a disdain for orthodoxy which is also a source of energy and a catalyst for questions. His energy, questioning and skills of engagement have enabled Ikeda and the creative people who work with him, not least his wife Kaneko, to share a journey in which he respects courtesies and customs but also challenges them, in which he acknowledges cultural constraints, yet is on the search for boundaries to be broken.

Boundaries broken

One part of my appraisal is complete. The man of stamina and vision, of commitment to engagement across countries and cultures, whose curiosity as a poet and photographer conveys a joy of life, does not appear to be unduly bothered by uncertainty. On the contrary he treats it as another challenge. The establishment of educational and cultural institutions displays the creative drive of someone who rises to challenges and brings others with him.

Universities and research centers in Japan and the United States, a Soka school system which provides a high standard of education, a diverse curriculum and inspiring extramural activities that operate in an imaginative and supportive atmosphere, testify to that creativity. That's not too surprising when the poet Ikeda can write of his hope, in his *Song of Youth*,

> that a myriad of flowers may bloom.
> out of the valley of darkness
> so that we may reach the high peaks of justice,
> from the rigid society of our times (Ikeda 1997, 15).

The crossing of boundaries requires not only courage but also a certain intellectual promiscuity allied to what I identify as street wisdom. The promiscuity refers to a desire to derive inspiration from any source. In Ikeda's case these sources have included photography, music, poetry and art. The street wisdom refers to the ability to obtain human, financial and material resources and then use them to good effect. A mix of people and disciplines, of political and administrative skills fires a creative spirit which sees the founding of the Institute of Oriental Philosophy in 1962, the Min-On Concert Association in 1963 and the Komeito political party the following year. This was followed by the building of the Tokyo Fuji Art Museum in 1983 and ten years later the establishment of the Boston Research Center for the 21st Century, later renamed the Ikeda Center for Peace, Learning and Dialogue. In 1996 Ikeda established the Toda Institute for Global Peace and Policy Research.

These educational and artistic accomplishments ran concurrent with the constant theme of moving his country and his people from a culture of violence to nonviolence, from concerns with militarism to a constant advocacy of peace. Commentary from an editorial in the *Japan Times* shows his fascination with dialogue as a driving force behind innovative meetings with people from all cultures: "It is crucial to revive the spirit of dialogue and to unleash a creative search for peaceful co-existence. To have faith in the promise of dialogue is to believe in the promise of humanity" ([2007] 2008, 81–2).

Initiatives in international relations

The encouragement of global citizenship through dialogue led to several initiatives in international relations. In 1968, at a time when China was considered an enemy of Japan and was isolated from the international community, Ikeda called for a restoration of Sino–Japanese ties. During the Cold War, influenced by his conviction that nuclear weapons are an absolute evil, he advocated "the need to create a global network of ordinary people for peace between the US and the USSR" (Urbain 2010, 149). This public stance came at a time when other leaders appeared to see only an impasse between East and West and rather than make overtures of friendship they relied on a build-up of arms as the best means of defense.

Ikeda's horror at the consequences of the dropping of the atomic bombs on Nagasaki and Hiroshima led to his lifelong advocacy of the abolition of nuclear weapons and pleas for a strengthening of the United Nations. Urbain observes that nuclear disarmament and UN reform appear in all of Ikeda's peace proposals. In the spirit of his concern with a common humanity, Ikeda sees the General Assembly of the UN as having the potential to be "a true parliament of humanity" but that potential is not realized because of the outdated veto powers of the five members of the Security Council.

Concerned about the UN's future, he has recommended the establishment of a "Council of World Citizens for the protection of the UN." Consistent with his commitment to global citizenship, Ikeda has also been an enthusiastic supporter of international institutions which constitute "elements of a global civilization" (Urbain 2010, 143), namely the International Criminal Court (ICC) and the International Atomic Energy Agency (IAEA).

Ikeda's focus on the need for peace in East Asia resulted in significant gestures of friendship, as in the creation of ties between Japan and other Asian countries and his repeated apologies for Japanese atrocities before and during World War II. In 1975 Soka University was the first to admit Chinese

students sponsored by the Chinese government. Ikeda has envisaged a North
East Asian Peace Community based on the European model and has called for
the reunification of the two Koreas.

The promise of biography

I finish this analysis by returning to "the promise of biography," the realizing
through diverse creative endeavors of all sorts of aspirations for the well-being
of others (Rees 1991). Ikeda has realized this promise in numerous ways and
has contributed to the happiness and fulfillment of millions. He has done
so by challenging conventions, by bringing people together and by mixing
disciplines. He is a leader who wants to be considered a private citizen but
conducts himself as an internationalist. He has been an astute politician and
sees the need for fundamental policy initiatives in Japan, overseas and in the
UN, yet can maintain "I am neither a politician nor a policy specialist."

A vision for the nobility of global citizenship, a joy for life expressed not
only through his advocacy of nuclear disarmament but also through inimit-
able poetry and photography, continues to drive Daisaku Ikeda. Throughout
his life he has had a sense of urgency that there is so much to be accomplished
and so little time to do it in. His hope and his vision remain firmly grounded
in the centrality of dialogue:

> The challenge of the 21st century
> is to firmly embrace this philosophy
> of fundamental humanism
> and to spread it throughout the world (Ikeda 2004b, 28).

Message to the Conference

The Power of Dialogue in a Time of Global Crisis

Daisaku Ikeda

On behalf of the Toda Institute for Global Peace and Policy Research, allow me to extend my warmest greetings to everyone gathered here today. I am both profoundly honored and grateful that so many scholars and activists of such great distinction have traveled from every corner of the world to take part in this international conference.

Twenty years have passed since the Cold War's demise. The ensuing march of globalization has been rapid, bringing about exchanges and encounters across a broad range of diverse realms. Yet it has also been cause for new tensions that fuel cycles of hatred and violence, culminating in further conflict and terrorism.

Exacerbating our predicament even further is the "trilemma" of global warming, the energy crisis and widespread food shortages, issues that feed off one another in an immense cycle of crises emerging concurrently around the globe.

And the most vulnerable states and peoples invariably suffer the worst of the repercussions. The global financial meltdown of 2008 has only made this point even more salient, exposing the true extent and gravity of global disparities.

Given the speed and scale with which the world's financial system proceeded to collapse, many voiced fears that we were on the threshold of another Great Depression. That calamity, which began in earnest in the 1930s, fanned widespread panic, forcing governments to adopt protectionist and other hard-line policies. The swift rise in xenophobia and racial bigotry that ensued, the crackdowns on freedom of thought – these factors eventually set the stage for World War II to erupt.

As Stefan Zweig noted in *The World of Yesterday*, "Contemporaries are denied a recognition of the early beginnings of the great movements which determine their times" (Zweig 1964, 362). Zweig wrote his autobiography as a caveat to the future, urging humankind never to repeat the errors of an age in which nations refused to reconcile their differences, while suppressing internal dissent.

While the crises we confront today may not share the same causes of our tragic past, their bitter lessons remain valid and vital. Nations must continue striving to open themselves up rather than close themselves off, as they are wont to do; they must seek to unite instead of divide, to create versus destroy, to work and prosper in harmony rather than allowing the strong to prey upon the weak. Only by effecting such a transition and collectively dedicating our strengths and resources can we prevail over the myriad global challenges thrust upon us.

The framework to achieve this – indeed, the very key to its success – lies with inter-civilizational dialogue, which has been and always will be a foundational objective of the Toda Institute. It is no coincidence that the United Nations has designated 2009 as the International Year of Reconciliation and 2010 as the International Year for the Rapprochement of Cultures. They attest to the imperative of the spirit of dialogue and tolerance to flourish in our world today.

This institute owes its roots to my mentor in life, Josei Toda, who strove mightily to "eliminate human misery from the face of the earth." His belief and struggle was grounded in the Buddhist spirit of compassion and empathy, which inspires one to share in the suffering of others and strive together to overcome them, so that we may all lead a life in the service of peace and individual happiness.

As with Zweig, Simone Weil's philosophical convictions were forged through the tragedy of war. Her insights resonate deeply with Buddhism, as is evident in the following passage:

And this same compassion is able, without hindrance, to cross fron-
tiers, extend itself over all countries in misfortune, over all countries
without exception; for all peoples are subjected to the wretchedness
of our human condition. Whereas pride in national glory is by its
nature exclusive, non-transferable, compassion is by nature universal
(Weil 2001, 172).

I believe it is the fundamental capacity of people to establish and expand
bonds of empathy that enables us to transcend through dialogue the walls of
religious differences, as well as the divisions between cultures and civilizations.

In ancient India, Shakyamuni Buddha's followers were called the *cātuddisa*
in Pali, or "people of four directions" who strove to broaden networks of
dialogue radiating outward to every corner of the world – a core tradition
of Buddhism. It was a tradition that Nichiren, the Buddhist teacher and
reformist of thirteenth-century Japan, underscored in his signal treatise,
"On Establishing the Correct Teaching for the Peace of the Land." In it, two
characters of markedly different social standing and disparate worldviews are
cast in fervid debate. They are compelled to do so out of a mutual desire to
better society and its multiplicity of miseries, examining the causes of human
suffering and possible solutions to alleviate them. Over the course of their
discussion, the two succeed in overcoming the divides that separate them
and the treatise concludes with their shared pledge to work for social change.
I embraced my mentor's impassioned call to banish human misery as my
own, leading me to engage in dialogue with individuals from a gamut of
cultural, religious and philosophical backgrounds, in a common quest to
resolve the most pressing issues of our day. I cherish the numerous associations
developed through these exchanges, which is why I am delighted by your participation in this conference and eagerly look forward to your contributions.
The path of dialogue that I have embarked upon so many years ago began
with an encounter with Arnold Toynbee. Convinced that history was shaped
by a process of "challenge and response," Dr. Toynbee made the following
observation: "Mankind's history is an Odyssey; we should be committing an
unforgivable sin against the innumerable generations still unborn if we were
to act, not like Odysseus, but like Ajax" (Toynbee 1992, 53).

As with Odysseus and his saga, we must also be prepared to persevere over repeated adversity, never to forego hope.

I firmly believe in the power of dialogue, that its prized sails and mighty oars will enable us to navigate through these perilous times, to impel humankind toward a global community of genuine peace and harmonious coexistence.

In closing, allow me to offer my heartfelt prayers for the great success of this conference and for the continued good health and myriad contributions of everyone here today.

November 22, 2009

Daisaku Ikeda, Founder
Toda Institute for Global Peace and Policy Research

Introduction

Olivier Urbain

As director of the Toda Institute for Global Peace and Policy Research, it gives me great delight to introduce this volume. The original inspiration for this book came from an international conference entitled "The Power of Dialogue in a Time of Global Crisis," held in Tokyo in November 2009, organized by the Toda Institute with the support of Soka University.

In the course of the conference, it appeared that we were pursuing at least two distinct purposes which sprang from the overall theme. First, we wanted to find ways to overcome the multiple crises affecting humanity as a whole, a set of global challenges that were exacerbated by the confrontation of various national and cultural interests. In this context, we wanted to explore the power of dialogue as a means to solve planetary problems, such as global poverty and environmental destruction. We wanted to explore what types of dialogue were needed to solve these issues concretely.

The second purpose was to focus on the ideas of Daisaku Ikeda, the founder of the Toda Institute, which has as its motto "Dialogue of Civilizations for Global Citizenship," by showing concrete examples of his actions for world peace for over half a century, a time during which the world has changed rapidly. The rate of globalization is accelerating every day, bringing a mixture of blessings and disasters, and we need powerful values and principles in order to counter its worst effects. For several decades, Ikeda has offered such a set of ideals, expressed in theory and demonstrated in practice, in order to build a more harmonious and peaceful world. He wrote in his 2009 Peace Proposal:

> At the most fundamental level, we must take initiatives to disrupt
> the cycle of violence and hatred and, in its place, build a robust

and pervasive culture of peace. We must ensure that every individual can enjoy in full the right to live in peace and dignity. For only this will serve as a solid safeguard for the world of the twenty-first century.

Dialogue presents infinite possibilities; it is a challenge that can be taken up by anyone – any time – in order to realize the transformation from a culture of violence to a culture of peace. It was based on this belief in the power of dialogue that, during the period 1974–75 as Cold War hostilities were intensifying, I made successive trips to China, the Soviet Union and the United States. As a concerned private citizen, I met with top-level leaders in each country in an effort to reduce and defuse tensions. Since that time, I have sought to counteract the forces of division by building bridges of friendship and trust around the world. (…)

If we allow ourselves to become confined within a certain ideology, ethnicity or religion – caught up in the kind of spirit of abstraction I discussed at the outset of this proposal – we will find ourselves at the mercy of the ebb and flow, stranded in the shallows of history, unable to make progress. In contrast, if we search beyond the arbitrary, surface labels and engage with each other as individuals in dialogue, generating spontaneous and intense interactions of heart and mind, we will be able to give rise to the "deeper, slower movements" which Toynbee considered to ultimately shape human history.

With this conviction, I have actively pursued dialogue with leaders and thinkers in various fields. Refusing to be deterred by the barriers dividing people, I have traveled between sometimes antagonistic societies, seeking to open lines of dialogue and communication where none had existed. Out of the desire to share the lessons learned through these dialogues as widely as possible, many of them have been published in book form (fifty thus far, with another twenty in preparation) (Ikeda 2009).

Concerning the first purpose, the results of our research were published in 2011 in the annual journal of the Toda Institute entitled *Peace & Policy*, volume 16, under the title "Empathetic Understanding and Virtuous Dialogue in a World of Risk and Uncertainty." The guest editor was Kevin Clements, Secretary-General of the Toda Institute, who is also Director of the National Center for Peace and Conflict Studies at the University of Otago, New Zealand. Besides the original papers from the conference, others were added after careful selection. Several noteworthy scholars have contributed to this issue, such as Nur Yalman, Professor of Social Anthropology and of Middle Eastern Studies at Harvard University and Sverre Lodgaard, Senior Research Fellow and former director of the Norwegian Institute of International Affairs (NUPI). This volume was also published in book form, augmented by additional chapters, under the title *Risk and Uncertainty: Understanding and Dialogue in the 21st Century*.

The current book is the result of collective discussions, research and writing on the second theme. It is also based on some of the papers presented at the 2009 Tokyo conference, with the addition of selected papers. A total of eight papers were carefully chosen, and they deal with the theory and practice of dialogue at different levels, inspired by the dialogical activities and writings of Ikeda, from the ideals found in ancient texts to citizen diplomacy, from interfaith meetings to small group discussions, from the design of university courses to the organization of exhibitions and networks. Authors come from various horizons, with activists such as Christine Atieno from Kenya, of the South–South Network, academics such as Wayne Hudson from Australia, Jason Goulah and Gonzalo Obelleiro from the US, and people who hold various positions in institutions established by Ikeda, such as Yoichi Kawada, Hirotomo Teranishi, Elizabeth Bowen and Kimiaki Kawai.

Ikeda's ideas on dialogue

Ikeda's principles for the construction of a peaceful and harmonious world and his actions based on dialogue are introduced succinctly and elegantly in the preface by Stuart Rees. Here I would like to explore and summarize some basic ideas found in Ikeda's philosophy of dialogue. The second half of the title of this book, "Dialogue for Peace," might seem to point to activities reserved to professional mediators, diplomats on the world stage, UN personnel and employees of other international and transnational organizations. However, this is not the intended meaning of the title of this volume.

Dialogue is an activity and a set of skills available to everyone, and the development of a culture of peace depends on the participation of as many people as possible in the process. Along these lines, Daisaku Ikeda said:

> Efforts to reach out and engage others in dialogue with the aim of fostering mutual understanding and bringing people closer together may seem ordinary and unexciting, but they in fact constitute a bold and daring challenge to create a new era of human civilization (Ikeda 2012).

This applies in conflict situations when agreements and solutions can be found through verbal exchanges, but also in the construction of a society based on a culture of peace. The relevance of dialogue for peacebuilding cannot be measured by standardized means. Any heart-to-heart dialogue between human beings can be said to contribute to a culture of peace.

In my book describing the philosophy of peace of Daisaku Ikeda (Urbain 2010), I highlighted how central the spirit and methodology of dialogue are to Ikeda's overall vision and sets of strategies for building a culture of peace. Ikeda often quotes authors who championed dialogue such as Socrates, Montaigne, Buber or Habermas. However, far from constituting abstract plans for the future of the world, Ikeda's practice of dialogue is acted out in very concrete and specific activities, spending time with a wide range of people, sometimes one individual at a time, sometimes with small groups, and sometimes with large audiences, in order to transform society and the human spirit through the practice of dialogue. The current volume is devoted to this transformative aspect of Ikeda's philosophy of dialogue.

While Ikeda constantly seeks to find common ground through his dialogues, he is also realistic about clarifying differences. Dialogue is not a way to remove differences in the hope that we will all merge into one happy organic whole, but an often paradoxical activity that implies a movement towards unity based on common ground, and at the same time a movement towards respectful distance based on the fact that no two human beings can completely agree on everything. Most of the time, there will be a point where people have to disagree. The art of dialogue can be defined as the ability to create meaningful and lasting understanding and relationships despite differences, and sometimes even thanks to these differences. For Ikeda, the driving force behind these efforts must be the type of humanism that allows us to find common ground and create lasting bonds between people:

> Seeking to look beyond national and ideological differences, I have engaged in dialogue with leaders in various fields from throughout the world. I have met and shared thoughts with people of many different philosophical, cultural and religious backgrounds, including Judaism, Christianity, Islam, Hinduism and Confucianism. My consistent belief, reinforced through this experience, is that the basis for the kind of dialogue required in the twenty-first century must be humanism – one that sees good in that which unites and brings us together, evil in that which divides and sunders us. (...)

> The real essence and practice of humanism is found in heartfelt, one-to-one dialogue. Be it summit diplomacy or the various interactions of private citizens in different lands, genuine dialogue has the kind of intensity described by the great twentieth-century humanist and philosopher Martin Buber (1878–1965) as an encounter "on the narrow ridge" in which the slightest inattention could result in a precipitous fall. Dialogue is indeed this kind of intense, high-risk encounter (Ikeda 2005, 2–3).

The chapters in this book

The book is divided into four sections of two chapters each. First some background is provided (Part 1), then a discussion on how Ikeda has applied Buddhist concepts to dialogue (Part 2), followed by an exploration of dialogue in education (Part 3), and finally the roles of dialogue in tackling global issues (Part 4).

Concerning the background, in chapter 1, "Philosophy of Peace in the Lotus Sutra," Yoichi Kawada explores the concept of peace in the Buddhist canon that serves as the basis for Nichiren Buddhism, and for Ikeda's Buddhist beliefs. The Lotus Sutra, one of the most important texts of Mahayana Buddhism, recommends the development of compassion for all, in line with what we call today a spirit of global citizenship, based on nonviolence and on the respect of each individual – the prerequisites for holding constructive dialogues for peace.

Three concepts which contribute to a philosophy of peace, and are essential in the development of global citizens, are "buddhahood in all people," which asserts that each human being has the potential for inherent goodness, the "eternal Buddha," meaning that all things in the universe are the workings of compassion, and "bodhisattva practice," praising those who help other people in many different ways and in fields such as science, the arts, medicine and information.

In chapter 2, "People Diplomacy: Daisaku Ikeda in China and the Former Soviet Union," Hirotomo Teranishi gives us information on the more high-profile dialogical activities of Ikeda, with intellectuals such as Count Coudenhove-Kalergi and Arnold Toynbee, heads of states such as Zhou Enlai and Aleksey Kosygin or high government officials such as Henry Kissinger. Teranishi shows that during a series of trips between Japan, China, the Soviet Union and the US in 1974–75, Ikeda was able to practice dialogue for peace in a way that had and still has long-lasting positive effects. For instance, many of the numerous exchange programs for students, academics and others between China and Japan can be traced back to the seeds planted at that time.

Concerning Buddhism in practice, in chapter 3, "Cosmopolitan Dialogue in an Interconnected, Ever-changing World," Gonzalo Obelleiro explores some core concepts of Buddhism that can be used to clarify the goals and methods of dialogue. He presents secular concepts such as cosmopolitan theory and humanitarian competition, as well as ideas at the core of the Buddhist worldview such as impermanence, interconnectedness, emptiness and the latent potential inherent in life, the middle way and the greater self.

In chapter 4, "Youth Perspectives: A Case Study of the Application in Australia of Group Dialogues for Peace," Elizabeth Bowen describes activities of the SGI in Australia, applying dialogue to the development of local groups, and in interfaith exchanges with Muslim youth. This chapter contains excerpts from actual interviews and constitutes a unique addition to this volume.

Concerning education, in chapter 5, "Daisaku Ikeda and Dialogue *on* Education, *in* Education and *as* Education," Jason Goulah highlights the similarities between Ikeda's use of dialogue and a Bakhtinian view of education. He identifies themes which are common to dialogue, peace and education, specifically analyzing Ikeda's dialogues with Russian, Chinese, Danish, North American and Taiwanese educators, and dedicates one section to a discussion with young people on bullying.

In chapter 6, "Daisaku Ikeda and Innovative Education," Wayne Hudson describes a course he taught using methodologies similar to those found in Ikeda's dialogues. He describes Ikeda's approach to dialogue as inclusive, correlationist and convergentist, and shows that it can be applied in the area of innovative education anywhere, beyond the context of Buddhism or of any particular religious organization.

Concerning global issues, in chapter 7, "Dialogical Approaches of Daisaku Ikeda and South–South Network," Christine Atieno discusses the similarities between the approaches of the South–South Network (SSN) and Ikeda's dialogical activities. She points out the different origins of the networks established by Ikeda and the SSN. Ikeda starts from a Buddhist point of view, his own wartime experiences, mentorship by Josei Toda, and the experience he gained by establishing numerous institutions that are meant to facilitate dialogue from the local to the global level. SSN was established in the framework of political and secular engagement, but Atieno finds many common points in the emphasis on respect for life and other values and principles in both organizations.

In chapter 8, "SGI's Dialogical Movement to Achieve a World without Nuclear Weapons," Kimiaki Kawai shows the links between Ikeda's stance towards nuclear abolition and his philosophy of dialogue. For instance, nuclear weapons and the theory of deterrence, based on a climate of mistrust and fear, are incompatible with human security and the purpose of dialogue. Another aspect is that through the consistent use of dialogue, human beings will be able to overcome the weaknesses of an international system that relies on nuclear weapons.

The power of dialogue and the creation of a new era

Here I want to highlight the overall vision that is expressed throughout this volume. It is the conviction that through dialogue we not only have the power to overcome the current crisis, but also to build a new era and a new society that would not be subject to the same type of crises. This can be accomplished through the kind of painstaking, and yet inspiring, paradigm shift proposed by Ikeda. In the 2009 Peace Proposal, he wrote:

> Dr. Toynbee warmly encouraged me to pursue dialogue when I met with him in 1972 and 1973. Viewing human history in terms of "challenge and response" with a perspective spanning centuries or millennia, he focused on the possibilities of dialogue rooted in our shared humanity as the driving force for creating a new era.
>
> Toynbee discussed the problem of human freedom in a lecture titled "Uniqueness and Recurrence in History" which he delivered in Japan in 1956. He noted that there appear to be laws governing the repetitive patterns in human history and extended this observation to the idea that civilizations have a life-cycle of approximately 800 years.
>
> However, he also emphatically asserted that certain human phenomena do not conform to such fixed patterns, concluding:
>
> "Of all human phenomena, the one for which no set pattern in fact exists is the field of encounter and contact between one personality and another. It is from such encounter and contact that truly new creativity arises" (Ikeda 2009).

I sincerely hope that this book will offer suggestions and be of help as we deepen our thinking in terms of the great prospect of "creating a new era," letting "new creativity" arise by multiplying and improving "encounter and contact between one personality and another."

As mentioned above, the promotion of "dialogue" is not only the responsibility of some people, such as political leaders, but requires the participation of all people on earth. This is how we can build a world where we can live harmoniously together as human beings, and with all other beings sharing our planet, with the dignity of each person shining brightly. If through some passages of this book readers feel encouraged in their search for such a society where meaningful and heart-to-heart dialogue becomes the norm, it will have fulfilled its purpose.

PART I

THE LOTUS SUTRA AND CITIZEN DIPLOMACY

CHAPTER 1

Philosophy of Peace in the Lotus Sutra

Yoichi Kawada

This world is like a burning house

The Simile and Parable chapter of the Lotus Sutra likens the phenomenal world to a "burning house," recounting how the Buddha appears in this world of suffering to save living beings. Even at the dawn of the twenty-first century humankind continues to repeat the destructive cycle of animosity and violence, and to suffer from the three poisons of hatred (rage), excessive desire (greed), and fundamental egoism (ignorance). The September 11, 2001 terrorist attacks in the first year of the new millennium were a historical occurrence painfully reminiscent of a well-known story in which "a fire suddenly broke out on all sides, spreading through the rooms of the house," as told in the Simile and Parable chapter of the sutra (Lotus Sutra 1993, 56). The terrorist acts led to a series of wars and conflicts, and the three poisons now threaten to engulf the entire world.

Soon after the September 11 tragedy, a collection of articles contributed by spiritual leaders around the world, representing Christianity, Islam, Judaism, Hinduism, and Buddhism, was published in the United States under the title *From the Ashes: A Spiritual Response to the Attack on America*. Daisaku Ikeda, president of the Soka Gakkai International, contributed an article entitled "The Evil over which We Must Triumph," in which he states that "international cooperation against terrorism cannot be limited to the short term. At a deeper level, it requires a profound reexamination of the nature of human civilization" (Ikeda 2001, 105–106). He calls for growth and development of the goodness inherent in human nature, saying:

> It is the function of evil to divide, to alienate people from each other and divide one country from another. The universe, this world, and our own lives are the stage for a ceaseless struggle between hatred and compassion, the destructive and constructive aspects of life (...)

> Unless we can achieve a fundamental transformation within our own lives, so that we are able to perceive an intimate connection with all our fellow human beings and feel their sufferings as our own, we will never be free of conflict and war. In this sense, I feel that a "hard power" approach, one that relies on military might, will not lead to a long-term, fundamental resolution (Ikeda 2001, 106).

Ikeda urges that inherent goodness be developed through inter-civilizational dialogue on all levels. Trying to solve problems through reliance on hard power such as military might is futile. The bloodshed and tragedy it causes only aggravates the reaction of hatred and rage. More integrated and multi-layered efforts should be made on various levels to generate a trend toward changing the violence of our times.

One such effort is aimed at strengthening international legal frameworks in order to prevent the spread of terrorism and conflict. Legal solutions should be sought through international legal institutions such as the International Criminal Court.

In order to grapple with the structural violence that broadly underlies direct violence, it is essential to promote human security, collaborating with various NGOs coordinated by the United Nations. Human security today requires not only protection of people by meeting their basic needs but also by increasing their skills and capacities, for people are the main engines of change.

In a complementary relationship with human security is "human development," which requires a philosophical and religious foundation upon which to cultivate goodness within human beings. Earthly passions should be conquered through innate goodness. One approach to the development of goodness is education; another is dialogue between civilizations and between religions. Education for peace, education for the environment, education for human rights, and so forth will help awaken the goodness inherent in the lives of children.

If education of this kind is sustained across the vertical axis of time, inter-civilizational and inter-religious dialogue spans the horizontal axis of space. Dialogue builds mutual trust and helps people to overcome their stereotypical and prejudiced views of civilization and religion; it helps them mutually recognize what is good that their civilizations and religions have in common. If we promote the common, universal features of humanity such as love, compassion, nonviolence, and morality, we can open up the way for destroying the "erroneous views" that encourage inter-religious and inter-civilizational divisiveness and conflict and for removing the hatred and enmity that such views generate.

I believe the most fundamental means of ensuring human security and development is promotion of dialogue and exchange on all levels – among heads of state, among specialists in various fields, and among ordinary people around the globe. Only when the current of dialogue for development of human goodness expands globally will legal, economic, and political measures be truly effective.

Philosophy of peace: Three key concepts in the Lotus Sutra

Here I introduce the three main concepts of the Lotus Sutra – "buddhahood in all people," "the eternal Buddha," and "bodhisattva practice" – and then discuss the idea of peace to which these concepts lead us. First, let us look at the concept of "buddhahood in all people." The Expedient Means chapter of the Lotus Sutra talks about the *ichidaiji innen*, or the sole purpose of the appearance of the Buddhas in this phenomenal world. They appear, it says, because they wish to "open" the door of Buddha wisdom to all living beings, "show" Buddha wisdom, "awaken" them to it, and induce them to "enter" the Buddha way (*kai-ji-go-nyu*) (Lotus Sutra 1993, 31). According to Chinese priest and scholar Tiantai (538–597) "Buddha wisdom" here means the same thing as Buddha nature.

From this passage, we can observe the following: (i) Buddhism affords the basis for human dignity; the reason human beings have dignity is because the "cosmic-scale life" (the Buddha wisdom, or Buddha nature), is inherent in the innermost depths of human life; (ii) the Lotus Sutra teaches that Buddha nature is inherent in every person, in all people, without distinction as to race, gender, ethnicity, cultural background, class, physical or psychological condition, occupation, and so forth; it thus makes the case for equality of all people; (iii) the idea of opening, showing, awakening, and inducing people to enter the Buddha way is a manifestation of the potential of human life, or full development of inherent goodness, abilities, sensitivity, and life energy; and (iv) the Parable of the Medicinal Herbs chapter of the Lotus Sutra relates how all plants and trees, which grow in the same earth and the same rain, each have their "differences and particulars" (Lotus Sutra 1993, 98), suggesting a principle for a peaceful society where all things coexist in harmony.

In a lecture given at Harvard University, SGI President Ikeda presented an image of the peaceful coexistence of all beings, saying:

> [This parable in the Lotus Sutra] symbolizes the enlightenment of all people touched by the Buddha's Law of great and impartial wisdom. At the same time, it is a magnificent paean to the rich diversity of humanity as well as all forms of sentient and insentient life, each equally manifesting the inherent enlightenment of its nature, each thriving and harmonizing in a grand concert of symbiosis (Ikeda 1993).

All beings developing their potential to the maximum equally sustained by the impartial workings of the universe; all people and nature breathing the Buddha life and demonstrating their individuality – this image of the sutra's parable evokes a peaceful society in which people live in harmony and prosperity with nature, a world where people have ceased destroying the environment and overcome direct and structural violence. Buddhism is a religion that aims to create such a society.

As for the "eternal Buddha," the second key concept, the Life Span of the Thus Come One chapter of the Lotus Sutra perceives Shakyamuni Buddha as a manifestation of the "Buddha from time without beginning," or the eternal Buddha (Lotus Sutra 1993, 225). In Buddhism, the universe was never created, and it will never end. The life of the universe is eternal and can be experienced by people here and now through chanting and other forms of meditation.

Shakyamuni as the eternal Buddha is one with the eternal Law and secures eternal salvation for all people. Shakyamuni guides people by various means, gives them benefits and salvation, and he has "never for a moment neglected" such acts of great compassion (Lotus Sutra 1993, 226). Josei Toda (1900–58), second president of the Soka Gakkai, talks about the salvation of the eternal Buddha who is one with the eternal Law from the viewpoint of cosmology, stating that salvation is the cosmic Buddha's practice of great compassion. He regards this universe entirely as the Buddha's substance, saying all things in the universe are the workings of compassion and that, therefore, compassion is the inherent nature of the universe. He describes the mission of humans, born in this universe, as follows:

> Inasmuch as the universe itself is compassion, our daily acts should naturally be acts of compassion. We lead special lives as humans, moreover; our position cannot be that of plants and animals. Lofty deeds are the work of those who truly serve the Buddha (Toda 1981, 45).

Toda adds, "We should live fully aware of the quality of true compassion" (Toda 1981, 48).

Toda explains the raison d'être and calling of humankind from Buddhism's cosmic perspective. In short, the "universal mission" of humans born on this planet is to take part in the cosmic workings of compassion and amplify them. Amplification of compassion means taking part in the creative evolution of the cosmos. In Mahayana Buddhism, those who practice this universal mission are bodhisattvas.

This brings us to the third key concept, or "bodhisattva practice." Let us look at bodhisattvas who appear in the Lotus Sutra – "bodhisattvas of the earth" (*jiyu no bosatsu*) and other bodhisattvas.

Bodhisattvas of the earth appear first in the Emerging from the Earth chapter of the Lotus Sutra as those who propagate the teachings of the sutra after Shakyamuni Buddha's passing. The Teacher of the Law chapter states that a person who expounds the sutra "is the envoy of the Thus Come One (…) dispatched by the Thus Come One and carries out the Thus Come One's work" (Lotus Sutra 1993, 162). This passage clearly shows the characteristics of bodhisattvas of the earth. These bodhisattvas are envoys of the Buddha following Shakyamuni Buddha's passing and perform the Buddha's work – salvation of humanity.

These bodhisattvas' work of compassion is seen in actual practice in the "burning house" of this phenomenal world. Such specific acts performed by other bodhisattvas are depicted from various angles in the Former Affairs of the Bodhisattva Medicine King and subsequent chapters. These are called "bodhisattvas of theoretical teaching" (*shakke no bosatsu*), the foremost of whom are the Medicine King (Yakuo), the Wonderful Sound (Myoon), the Universal Worthy (Fugen), and the Perceiver of the World's Sounds (Kannon), working in medicine, art, science, and information, respectively. Amid the "burning house," the Medicine King takes charge of freedom from illness, securing food, water, medicine, and health, and displaying the rights of people who pray for health and longevity. The bodhisattva Wonderful Sound asserts the freedom of artistic expression as represented by music, and the bodhisattva Universal Worthy proclaims freedom of thought and learning.

The bodhisattva who listens to people's earnest wishes, fulfills those wishes, and brings people into a "fear not" state is the Perceiver of the World's Sounds, who is also called *Semui-sha* (Bestower of Fearlessness). The actual content of salvation secured by this bodhisattva takes the form of benefits obtained in this world. In this mundane world, which is in the state of a burning house, perceiving and meeting the needs of people is what constitutes human security.

Qualities of global citizens:
Bodhisattva Never Disparaging as a model

In the Lotus Sutra, a specific behavior of the bodhisattvas of the earth can be best found in the bodhisattva Never Disparaging, whom Shakyamuni identifies as himself in a previous existence. In the Bodhisattva Never Disparaging chapter, at a time when arrogant monks were a dominant force, a bodhisattva named Never Disparaging appeared and revered everyone he met, saying, "I would never dare treat you with disparagement or arrogance. Why? Because you are all practicing the bodhisattva way and are certain to attain Buddhahood" (Lotus Sutra 1993, 266–67).

The behavior of the bodhisattva depicted in the sutra suggests to us ways we should behave as global citizens. First, the reason the bodhisattva reveres everyone is because, even if he finds them to be arrogant on the surface, he reveres the Buddha nature that shines inside them. He preaches that, by practicing the bodhisattva way, people can manifest their Buddha nature and fully enjoy a great state of Buddhahood brimming with goodness of heart. Second, the bodhisattva Never Disparaging is committed to nonviolence as a means of manifesting his Buddha nature. The only way for us to manifest from our innermost depth the great life of the eternal Buddha is to devote ourselves to nonviolence. It is impossible to manifest the Buddha world by means of violence and enmity. And third, when he is about to die, the bodhisattva Never Disparaging hears the voice of a Buddha, which purifies his life force and extends his life span. This is the best example of the Buddha world becoming manifest in one's last moments and one's Buddha nature coming into full bloom. The life energy of the Buddha world extends the Never Disparaging bodhisattva's life, and he devotes that extended life to salvation of others through nonviolent means.

It is global citizens who are the driving force behind the movement for nonviolence. In conclusion, therefore, let me sum up several qualities of global citizens as suggested by the Lotus Sutra.

First, global citizens are those who embrace a view of life that supports the dignity of humankind and the sanctity of life. The Life Span chapter emphasizes this dimension by way of the Buddha as eternal savior, namely the eternal Buddha who is at one with the eternal Law.

Second, global citizens should manifest the Buddhahood inherent within themselves based on the idea of the Buddha as eternal savior, as shown in the Expedient Means chapter. The respect of global citizens for human dignity is an embodiment of the idea that all people are equally equipped with the Buddha nature regardless of race, gender, ethnicity, cultural background, occupation, or social standing, and the implementation of that idea.

Third, global citizens are committed to nonviolence, as the behavior of the bodhisattva Never Disparaging suggests. They should not use violence as a means for improving the world, but develop, with wisdom and compassion, nonviolent means, such as dialogue, face-to-face or communication exchange, proactive participation, education, culture, and awareness-raising.

Fourth, for global citizens, self-actualization is found in work for the benefit of others and in doing their best to save all humanity and bring an everlasting peace to planet Earth. As described in the Lotus Sutra, the bodhisattva way consists of performing the universal mission, or salvation of all humanity. World citizens, having been born in this world, should be aware of their mission and cultivate their lives in order to fulfill it.

Fifth, as the Parable of the Medicinal Herbs chapter conveys the image that all plants and trees, which grow in the same earth and are nourished by the same rain, each have their differences, global citizens should aspire to the peaceful coexistence of diverse cultures – an ideal state of "all for one, one for all." That is the society where all its members display their characteristics and develop their latent talents and abilities while maintaining a symbiotic integrity within that dynamic harmony.

Sixth, global citizens, who take the lead in creating a multicultural society of coexistence as described above, should have a pluralistic identity of self. Like bodhisattvas in the Lotus Sutra, they should be able to adapt themselves to whatever situation they might be in so that they can flexibly serve others. The Bodhisattva Wonderful Sound and Bodhisattva Perceiver of the World's Sounds, for example, manifest themselves, respectively, in 34 and 35 different forms in accordance with the particular suffering people are facing.

Seventh, the bodhisattva-like self of a global citizen is a multi-layered, dynamic, and integrated self consisting of an "ethnic self," "national self," and "global self." In his book *A Geography of Human Life*, Tsunesaburo Makiguchi (1871–1944), the first president of the Soka Gakkai, discusses the plurality of the self of all people, who are at the same time citizens of the homeland, of the nation, and of the world, in what he calls a "multilayered worldview" (Makiguchi 2002). The homeland is where you are living now, and by solidly observing that local place you can broaden your perspective, first to "nation" and "country," and then become aware of your being one of the countless global citizens living in coexistence with Nature, says Makiguchi. He empha-sizes experience with the homeland because a person whose perspective begins from the homeland will look at the world from a perspective firmly rooted in the local.

The bodhisattva-like self will broaden one's homeland experience and, as a member of one's nation and then as a fully global citizen, one will act in the different places where one finds oneself, and in fields where one's latent abilities can be best displayed. All the qualities of a global citizen described above are encompassed by the universal mission of saving all humanity and of utilizing nonviolence and compassion as means to fulfill that objective. It is global citizens committed to this mission and nonviolent means who will create the everlasting peace demonstrated in the Lotus Sutra.

CHAPTER 2

People Diplomacy: Daisaku Ikeda in China and the Former Soviet Union

Hirotomo Teranishi

Introduction

Over the years I have had an opportunity to meet Daisaku Ikeda and to accompany him abroad on numerous occasions. I have always been impressed with his commitment to, and talent for, dialogue, be it with ordinary members of the Buddhist lay organization Soka Gakkai International, or with world-famous intellectuals and politicians. In this chapter I would like to share my impressions concerning historical facts related to Ikeda's most high-profile dialogues, namely with intellectuals such as Count Coudenhove-Kalergi and Arnold Toynbee, with heads of state such as Zhou Enlai and Aleksey Kosygin or politicians such as Henry Kissinger. I am convinced that these dialogues have changed the course of history for the better.

Buddhist activities

In 1960, at the young age of 32, Ikeda became the third president of the lay Buddhist organization, Soka Gakkai. In the same year he took his first step into the world, visiting nine cities in North, Central, and South America, organizing and encouraging Soka Gakkai members in each region. By 1967, he had made a total of 13 overseas trips. The main purpose of these trips was to help overseas Soka Gakkai members to organize their activities.

Records of Ikeda's activities during this period show that he frequently conferred with overseas journalists. In these conferences, journalists were addressing the leader of a rapidly growing Soka Gakkai, showing particular interest in his reasons for founding the Komeito, a political party, in 1964. However, his meetings with Count Coudenhove-Kalergi that took place in 1967 and 1970 were of a different nature. These meetings covered subjects such as a comparison of the cultures of East and West and discussions on the future direction the world ought to take. This may be considered Ikeda's first full-fledged exchange of views with the international intelligentsia.

Toynbee

During a visit to Japan in 1967, the historian Arnold Toynbee expressed his wish to engage in a dialogue with someone representing the Mahayana Buddhist philosophy. Regarding his selection of Daisaku Ikeda – still in his 40s at the time – as his counterpart representing the Mahayana philosophy, we can find an explanation in the following statement by Takeo Kuwabara (Honorary Professor of Kyoto University), who assisted with the Japanese translation of Toynbee's famous work *A Study of History* and who also engaged in a dialogue with the historian in 1967: "Western thinkers tend to have a much stronger interest in the Soka Gakkai than Japanese intellectuals. This is because they come from a context where religion has often been a force of resistance against political power, unlike Japan whose religious community has been emasculated by political power. Mr. Toynbee was one such person" (Kuwabara 1976). According to Kuwabara, then, Toynbee was eager to meet the leader of a religious organization that was active in the Japanese society of the time.

Reading the two dialogues gives me a strong sense of Toynbee's profound concern about the crisis facing our contemporary society, his critical attitude toward the Christian civilization that brought about this predicament, and his enthusiastic pursuit of the Mahayana philosophy. In their dialogue Toynbee asks Ikeda for confirmation on various aspects of Mahayana Buddhism. I believe he chose Ikeda not as a theoretician but as a practitioner, and that he did this in order to confirm his understanding – the result of his personal pursuit and studies. Ikeda can indeed be considered as a "practitioner" of Mahayana Buddhism.

During the period from 1968 to 1971, Ikeda did not travel. This coincides with the successive openings of Soka Gakuen (1968) and Soka University (1971). It was at this time that he received a letter from Toynbee, requesting a dialogue. The letter received in the autumn of 1969 said:

> When I was last in Japan in 1967, people talked to me about the Sokagakkai [sic] and about you yourself. I have heard a great deal about you. (…) I am going to read some of your books and speeches translated into English. (…) It is my pleasure, therefore, to extend to you my personal invitation to visit me in Britain in order to have with you a fruitful exchange of views on a number of fundamental problems of our times which deeply concern us all (Kelly 2002, 20 quoted in Seager 2006, 117).

Ikeda accepted the invitation, and the dialogue started in May 1972. After a total of ten days of dialogue over a period of two years, the book *Man Himself Must Choose* was published in 1974 (the title was later changed to *Choose Life*). The preface reads:

> Toynbee's fear that the next chapter of history may be more violent and brutal than Ikeda thinks that it need be is the difference between the religious traditions in which the two authors have been brought up. Toynbee was brought up as a Christian; Ikeda is a Buddhist of the Northern (Mahayana) school. Both Buddhism and Christianity have spread widely (more widely than any non-religious institution so far), but the means and the consequences of their dissemination have differed. Buddhism, which has spread almost exclusively by peaceful penetration, has been content to coexist amicably with the other religions and philosophies that it has found already present in the regions in which it has been propagated. (…) In spite of the difference between the authors' religious and cultural backgrounds, a remarkable degree of agreement in their outlooks and aims has been

brought to light in their dialogue. Their agreement is far-reaching (Toynbee and Ikeda 1976, 10–11).

Toynbee believed that besides enabling them to reach agreements that were far-reaching, the dialogue was also of great importance for the future of the world. Upon hearing the news on May 19, 1973 – the last day of the dialogue – that the Soviet General Secretary Leonid Brezhnev was visiting West German Prime Minister Willy Brandt and had held an historic conference, Toynbee stated that "while his dialogue with [Ikeda] might not attract as much attention as a summit meeting, what they were doing was for the benefit of future generations. With earnest conviction, he added that he believed dialogues like his and [Ikeda]'s were the key to building a path to lasting peace" (Ikeda 2008, 165). And at the end of the dialogue, Toynbee expressed his hope that Ikeda would continue to engage in this kind of dialogue, handing him a memo with the names of seven people. With due consideration to such exchange, I am convinced that the dialogue with Toynbee was a major turning point in Ikeda's concrete activities for the realization of world peace.

In January 1974, Ikeda visited Hong Kong, then North, Central and South America in March and April. His first visit to China was from May 29 to June 16, and it was followed by his first visit to the Soviet Union from September 8 to 18, and then China again from December 2 to 6. In the following year, he visited the United States in January, made a third trip to China in April, and then visited the United Kingdom, France, and the Soviet Union in May. During all of these trips, he visited various universities, delivered lectures, and conferred with numerous distinguished people. I would now like to focus on the highlights of his travels to China and the Soviet Union.

China

With regard to China, Ikeda's 1968 proposal appealing for the normalization of China–Japan relations and for China to assume its rightful position in the international community – in other words to acquire official representation in the United Nations – is well known. This proposal reflects Ikeda's belief based on his holistic/historic perspective that peace in Asia and in the world cannot be achieved without normalizing relations with China, a major country with a population of over 700 million at that time. Also, when Ikeda founded the Komeito Party in 1964, he suggested including in the Party's program the political issue of normalizing relations with China. In those days, in submission to US policy, Japan recognized Taiwan as the only China, and in later years it was rumored that one of the officials of the Ministry of Foreign Affairs had mentioned to the US government that the Japanese government was annoyed that such a proposal had been made by a simple civilian. Furthermore, after the issuance of this proposal, many right-wing activists publicly attacked Ikeda. In this light, Premier Zhou Enlai and other Chinese officials regarded this courageous action highly. Upon receiving an invitation from the Chinese government, Ikeda asked Komeito, the party he had founded, to work for the normalization of China–Japan relations. And finally, based on prior negotiations, Prime Minister Kakuei Tanaka visited China in September 1972 to officially establish bilateral relations.

Following this event, Ikeda's visit to China was realized in May 1974. Prior to this trip, Ikeda conferred with then Chinese Ambassador Chen Chu and met with Soviet Ambassador Alexander Troyanovsky in Tokyo to discuss his scheduled visit to China and the Soviet Union. These conferences right before his trip to China and his scheduled visit to the Soviet Union in autumn of the same year reflect Ikeda's profound concern about the growing tensions between the two countries. The growing bilateral tensions – born of differences in policies since 1956 and the arrest of Soviet helicopter pilots who had been accused of spying after straying into Chinese territory – implied an imminent escalation into war. With a successful nuclear test in 1964 making China a nuclear power, Ikeda recognized the possibility that nuclear weapons may be deployed in the event of a war between the two countries.

On May 30, 1974, Ikeda and his delegation crossed the border by foot from Hong Kong to Shenzhen and stayed in China for 17 days. This was his first trip to China. He traveled to the six cities of Beijing, Xi'an, Zhengzhou, Shanghai, Hangzhou, and Guangzhou. During his stay he visited Beijing University, meeting with Vice Premier Li Xiannian, and toured various schools and factories, thus promoting exchanges with people from various walks of life. During this sojourn, he was not able to meet with Premier Zhou Enlai as the Chinese Premier had just had surgery. However, every detail of Ikeda's activities was reported to him.

There are three prime points to be noted regarding this trip. The first point is Ikeda's enthusiastic challenge to promote exchange with Chinese people. This may be exemplified by a conversation between Ikeda and a little girl. On the occasion of the Beijing Children's Festival, a little girl who escorted Ikeda asked, "Why did you come to China?" and Ikeda responded, "I came to see you." The second is that during this sojourn, in his talks with officials of the China–Japan Friendship Association and government officials, Ikeda expressed his views frankly on matters such as the issue of nuclear weapons and diplomatic policies for achieving world peace. And third, when he saw shelters being constructed against a Soviet attack in junior high schools and urban areas in Beijing, he was convinced of the dire necessity of alleviating tensions between these two countries. On the final day of his visit to China, he conferred with Vice Premier Li Xiannian for two hours and 15 minutes, during which the vice premier confirmed that China would not preemptively use nuclear weapons and would firmly defend the five principles of peace.

During this trip, Ikeda began to write about what he saw in China, and upon his return to Japan – in spite of his busy schedule – published these articles in July and August in major Japanese weekly and monthly magazines. In December, these articles were also published in book form by Mainichi Shimbun under the title *Human Revolution in China*.

The Soviet Union

In September of the same year, Ikeda together with a Soka University delegation visited the then Soviet Union for the first time. When this news became known, many criticized him, saying "what is the leader of a religious organization doing in a communist country?" I was a freshman at Soka University, established by Ikeda in 1971, in those days. I vividly remember right-wing students who opposed Ikeda's trip to the Soviet Union intruding into our campus during the night, scattering flyers denouncing his visit. I assume that this kind of antagonistic attitude existed not only in Japan but also in the Soviet Union.

During this visit, Vice Rector Vladimir Ivanovich Tropin welcomed Ikeda to Moscow State University and accompanied him at almost all events. Reflecting on his memories of Ikeda in the Soviet Union, he published the book *Twenty Years of Encounters* in 1995, in which he vividly describes Ikeda's meetings with numerous people in the Soviet Union. His portrayal of the meeting with Premier Aleksey Kosygin at the Kremlin is particularly interesting. The vice rector writes that Premier Kosygin is the kind of person who is uncompromisingly realistic. He did not expect anything from Ikeda and so expected this meeting to be a simple courtesy call that would last only a few minutes before the premier would give the signal to end the conversation. Nevertheless, in reality the discussion was a very humane exchange of views that lasted well beyond the scheduled time.

Until this meeting, whenever Premier Kosygin had met with a delegate from Japan, all they would discuss was the northern territories. He never expressed any desire for an improvement in Soviet–Japan relations. On the other hand, Ikeda talked about his and the Japanese people's respect for Russian literature, folk songs, ballet, and music. Ikeda also gave his impressions of Leningrad, the birthplace of the Premier, and with reference to the struggle against fascism, expressed his strong desire for a world without war. He also conveyed a message from Premier Li Xiannian that he had been entrusted to deliver during his visit to China (that China would not preemptively use nuclear weapons and would firmly defend the five principles of peace), and communicated the Chinese people's yearning for peace. Ikeda continued, appealing for the promotion of a bilateral exchange of culture and education and for further mutual understanding.

When the subject of armaments came up, it is said that Premier Kosygin expressed his serious concern, saying that "today, weapons have been developed that can eradicate the human race in an instant, and there is no guarantee that the world can survive." These words completely contradicted the conventional theory that the Soviet nuclear arsenal guaranteed world peace. In a nutshell, the Premier had clearly stated that the world definitely should not be threatened by nuclear weaponry, that the Soviet Union would never do such a thing, nor would it attack China or isolate that country from the international community. In his book, the vice rector describes the unexpected development arising out of this meeting with an individual civilian, which astounded all of the attendees at the conference.

During this trip, Ikeda conversed enthusiastically with the people. As was the case with his visit to China, he also wrote his impressions of this visit – which were published after his return to Japan. In February of 1975, these writings were published as a book titled *My Soviet Diary*. Be it China or the Soviet Union, the differences in governmental systems meant that the Japanese had no way of truly knowing the people living there. By conveying the casual words of ordinary people expressing their desire for peace – both in China and the Soviet Union – Ikeda vividly portrayed that they are no different from us. This was an expression of his conviction that peace cannot be realized without mutual understanding.

Back to China

In December of 1974, at the invitation of Beijing University, Ikeda traveled to China for the second time. He conferred with Vice Premier Deng Xiaoping and conveyed a message from Kosygin. On the same day at around midnight, Premier Zhou Enlai went against the opinion of his advisors and met with Ikeda even though he was hospitalized at the time. At the meeting, Zhou Enlai thanked Ikeda for his contribution to the normalization of Sino–Japan relations and said, "You are still young. I entrust to you the task of promoting Sino–Japan friendship." In response to this man of outstanding stature in the history of China and the world, who insisted on meeting him, Ikeda has consistently continued to appeal for Sino–Japan friendship. He has now made a total of 11 trips to China, continuing to promote friendship with successive Chinese leaders even to this day.

It is worth mentioning how Soka University has contributed to Sino–Japanese friendship. In a message about the Beijing office of Soka University, University President Hideo Yamanoto stated:

> Soka University was the first in Japan to receive six students from China on a Chinese government program launched after the nor-malization of bilateral diplomatic relations in 1972. Our institution was the first in Japan to conclude an official agreement of academic exchange with Peking University in 1979, enjoying similar agree-ments of academic exchange with over 30 Chinese universities since then. Based on the above-mentioned exchange agreements, Soka University has received more than 160 visiting faculty members and

researchers from China and sent over 600 Soka students to various
Chinese universities (Soka University website).

As an ordinary citizen, Ikeda has continued to engage in frank and honest
dialogues with the leaders of both China and Russia, fostering mutual trust
and doing whatever he could to promote direct dialogue. Needless to say, on
his numerous returns to these countries he has been promoting educational
and cultural exchanges in a variety of ways through Soka University and the
Min-on Concert Association that he founded. After 1975, Sino–Soviet relations did not improve overnight but no serious armed conflict developed.
From 1982, the countries started to gradually but mutually soften their
stances, and finally in May of 1989, President Mikhail Gorbachev visited
China and met with Premier Deng Xiaoping, declaring a normalization of
relations.

The United States

In January of 1975, Ikeda visited the United States and met with then UN
Secretary-General Kurt Waldheim and Secretary of State Henry Kissinger.
In these meetings, he also related his discussions with the leaders of both
China and the Soviet Union. This was followed by a visit to Guam, where
he founded the Soka Gakkai International (SGI) and held the First World
Peace Conference, with the participation of representatives from 51 countries.
SGI upholds the objective of forming a solidarity that transcends borders
to address the various problems facing the world such as issues of nuclear
armament, the environment, and the North–South divide. From 1960, when
he became president of Soka Gakkai, Ikeda addressed the representatives of
each national SGI organization, encouraging and fostering all of them. He
spoke of his dialogue with Toynbee, covering subjects related to the future of
humanity and the crisis of imminent war in the contemporary world.

It is my belief that the basis of what Ikeda terms "humanitarian diplomacy"
lies in a strong awareness of human existence in promoting diplomacy among
countries pursuing peace. In other words, the heads of state representing
each country – while working to further the interests of their own states
and establishments – should not lose sight of what it is to be an individual

human being. It is based on this recognition that Ikeda continues to repeat-edly emphasize the importance of direct and honest exchanges of views among heads of states. Moreover, in any nation's decision-making process the impor-tance of promoting mutual understanding on a large scale – at the people's level – should also not be forgotten. For this reason, Ikeda strives tirelessly in his writings to portray the true image of the people. Above all, by promoting the SGI movement throughout the world, he is endeavoring to enlarge the circle of solidarity of people who share his conviction.

Conclusion

While most of us will not have an opportunity to meet with such renowned world figures as those mentioned in this chapter, I believe each of us has a mission to use dialogue in order to spread mutual understanding and respect for life. It is through careful attention to detail and focused engagement that Ikeda has been able to accomplish so much through dialogue, and I believe anybody can use the same conviction to reach meaningful results.

PART II

BUDDHISM AS A PRACTICAL
PHILOSOPHY OF DIALOGUE

Chapter 3

Cosmopolitan Dialogue in an Interconnected, Ever-changing World

Gonzalo Obelleiro

Introduction

Dialogue can be regarded as a method for conflict resolution, as pedagogic strategy, as a way of interacting with the world. Daisaku Ikeda has extensively written on and engaged in dialogue in all these modes. One particular perspective is recurrently explored in Ikeda's writings on dialogue: that of dialogue as a way of learning from those who are different. Dialogue as learning across difference is a central theme of cosmopolitanism. For Ikeda, an avowed cosmopolitan, dialogue is at the heart of his philosophy of global citizenship. In this chapter I explore Ikeda's philosophy of dialogue from a cosmopolitan perspective.

As Richard Seager (2006) argues, global citizenship and dialogue have been instrumental to the development of Ikeda's thinking. Ikeda's interpretation of Buddhism grew from within the process of spreading the teachings of Nichiren Buddhism outside Japan. This has been, since the outset, a process involving a conscious engagement in dialogue across differences. Dialogue is not only one of the central themes in Ikeda's writings, but also a method for the development of the philosophy itself. Commentators have also identified the centrality of cosmopolitanism and dialogue in Ikeda's philosophy of peace (Urbain 2010), and his philosophy of education (Miller 2002; Ikeda 2006, 2010; Goulah 2012).

After a brief overview of contemporary scholarship on cosmopolitanism, I explore Ikeda's philosophy of dialogue from the opposing perspectives that characterize the encounter with normative tension: collaboration and competition. I call them the *empathetic* and the *agonistic* functions of dialogue. From these two functions of dialogue I explore connections with an ontology of interconnectedness and impermanence found in the Buddhist concept of the *three perceptions*. I then propose three dimensions of dialogue in Ikeda: dialogue as discipline of persistence, dialogue beyond concepts, and dialogue as artful practice. Finally, I conclude by pointing to the Buddhist notion of the *greater self* as moral ideal and response to the challenges of a world of irreducibly conflicting values.

Contemporary scholarship on cosmopolitan theory

Contemporary scholarship on cosmopolitanism often comes with a description of the human condition in the twenty-first century as defined by intensified interconnectedness and ever more rapid rate of change. Nel Noddings articulates it eloquently:

> In a world of instant communication and swift travel, we have become keenly aware of our interdependence. Many of us are now concerned about the welfare of all human and non-human life, preservation of the Earth as home to that life, and the growing conflict between the appreciation of diversity and the longing for unity. We are concerned, too, that our technological capacity has run far beyond our moral competence to manage it. We dream of peace in a world perpetually on the edge of war (Noddings 2005, 1).

These images of increased interconnectedness accompanied by a weighty sense of moral responsibility make reference to ideas that are "in the air." Rather than expressing an idiosyncratic point of view, Noddings articulates commonly held beliefs about the nature of our times.

In response to the challenges Noddings describes, cosmopolitanism is conceived as an ethical and moral orientation to confront an increasingly interconnected and ever-changing world (Hansen 2008a, 2008b, 2010a, 2010b, 2011; Strand 2010a, 2010b). But as much as it is true that we live in times marked by exponential advances in communications technologies, a deep sense of our interconnectedness has long been part of our condition. The idea of cosmopolitanism is, not surprisingly, also millennia old. Its basic tenet is that we ought to regard all of humanity as belonging to a single community.

The past 15 years have seen a flourishing of research on cosmopolitanism across fields (Hansen 2010a; Hansen 2010b; Strand 2010b; Todd 2010). Some theorists even refer to our time in history as marked by a "cosmopolitan turn in the social and political sciences" (Strand, 2010a), and as existentially defined by a "cosmopolitan condition" (Strand 2010a; Beck 2006; Beck and Sznaider 2006; Delanty 2006; Pieterse 2006). More simply, scholars claim, we live in a world where the cosmopolitan question cannot be ignored.

Cosmopolitan thinking today is much different from that of modernity. While modernist debates were "fueled by antinomies such as engagement versus estrangement, patriotism versus universalism, sentiment versus detached reason," contemporary debates operate within a framework of "a dialectic that resolves such antinomies" (Gregoriou 2003, 257). Contemporary cosmopolitanisms are not about exchanging values rooted in our local cultures for loyalty to universal values; they are not about unreflectively choosing the well-being of humanity as a whole over that of our family members and compatriots. Instead, contemporary cosmopolitanisms recognize the value of particular cultures and local commitments; they value diversity. At the same time, they appreciate the urgent need to work together across differences.

Because cosmopolitanism recognizes the value of both local and global commitments, of particular and universal values, it "positions [people] to dwell meaningfully in the tension-laden, often paradoxical realm of being both destabilizers and preservers of culture. Individuals and communities destabilize culture every time they learn something genuinely new and different" (Hansen 2008a, 206). Dialogue from a cosmopolitan perspective, then, becomes an approach to inhabiting the normative tensions of the world.

Across the broad spectrum of different versions of contemporary cosmopolitanism, dialogue figures prominently in most. Martha Nussbaum, for example, considers that the moral stance of a cosmopolitan entails "work[ing] to make all human beings part of our community of dialogue and concern"

(Nussbaum 1996, 9). Seyla Benhabib (2006) proposes a cosmopolitanism based on what she calls "democratic iterations," in which dialogue at different levels of democratic participation is central. Kwame Anthony Appiah summarizes his philosophy of global citizenship in three basic principles: "(1) we don't need a single world government, but (2) we must care for the fate of all human beings, inside and outside our own societies, and (3) we have much to gain from conversation with one another across differences" (Appiah 2008, 87). Even in this most succinct articulation, dialogue appears as central.

Dialogue, empathy, and our shared humanity

One of the functions of dialogue is to provide conditions for individuals to transcend differences and bring out a sense of shared humanity. The focus is on cultivating conditions for individuals to recognize in the other, above anything else, a fellow human being. And through this recognition, in turn, to see themselves in the same light: as a human individual. I call this the *empathetic function of dialogue*. Ikeda makes it central and explicit in his many encounters with political, academic and intellectual leaders.

For example, in *Creating Waldens*, the published version of his dialogue with American Renaissance scholars Ronald Bosco and Joel Myerson, within the first few pages Ikeda directs the conversation to a discussion about his interlocutors' youth and the path that led them to their current work: "Let me ask both of you to share some memories of your youth and describe how you came to research Thoreau." He then asks personal questions about his interlocutors' lives: "Dr. Bosco, I understand that your family emigrated from Italy. What part of Italy? What were your parents like?" (Bosco et al. 2009, 7), and "Dr. Myerson, what did you learn from your parents?" (Ibid., 9). In his dialogue with Prof. Majid Tehranian, he makes a similar move. After a brief exchange about the general topic of peace and security, Ikeda asks his interlocutor about his personal life:

> Before we begin our discussion, I would like to ask you about your personal background. That will help deepen our mutual understanding and it will also be a good way to introduce you to our readers (Tehranian and Ikeda 2011, 2).

We notice that, in this case, he explicitly states the purpose of these personal questions: "deepen our mutual understanding." Urbain (2010) argues that by asking "personal questions at the beginning (...) [Ikeda] propels the dialogue to a more profound level" and that the significance of these exchanges around personal questions "lies in the sense of intimacy these personal details have created between Ikeda and his partners" (Urbain 2010, 129). I agree with Urbain.

The "mutual understanding" and "sense of intimacy" that Ikeda seeks to establish early in an exchange have a philosophical significance beyond merely creating comfortable conditions for conversation. For Ikeda, even when he recognizes that there are historical, cultural and moral barriers that separate people, there is also a human nature that we share. In his "Education Toward Global Citizenship," he characterizes global citizenship in terms of

(1) The wisdom to perceive the interconnectedness of all life and living; (2) The courage not to fear or deny difference, but to respect and strive to understand people of different cultures and to grow from encounters with them; (3) The compassion to maintain an imaginative empathy that reaches beyond one's immediate surroundings and extends to those suffering in distant places (Ikeda 2010, 112–13).

This vision of global citizenship can also be articulated in terms of one's relationship with our shared humanity. We could say that the wisdom of the global citizen lies in recognizing this shared humanity. The courage of the global citizen lies in not fearing the diversity that is inherent to our humanity, but learning from it. The compassion of the global citizen lies in caring about a single individual as human being. In seeking to establish a personal connection at the outset of a dialogue, Ikeda strives to embody the virtues of the global citizen. He tries to engage, not the scholar, the political leader, the Westerner, the representative of this or that religion, but the human being in front of him.

Sarah Wider offers an eloquent and insightful account of Ikeda's attitude in dialogue:

Societal distinctions can exert tremendous power over others, abusing the powerful connections that fundamentally establish mutual and just relations. Whether through his writings, through our face-to-face conversations or in his ongoing dialogues, I have seen how President Ikeda meets people. He greets the person, not their societal role. He's not speaking to the title or the perceived place in society that person holds. He speaks to the person, to the complex human being, and not simplistically to "the doctor," "the cashier," "the athlete," "the professor," "the janitor" (Wider and Yokota 2010).

What Wider describes as "the person" and "the complex human being" is, for Ikeda, not an abstract notion of universal humanity. We do not find what we all share by means of abstracting away our particularities and reaching a universal that lies high above ground. Rather, we find what we all share by going lower, by digging deeper towards the common *ground* of our most basic needs of nourishment, care, health, safety, and meaning. Ikeda's archetype of the global citizen is not the rational philosopher or the world-traveling financier, but the mother who cares about her child and who understands another mother from a different culture who also cares about her child.

The foreword to *The World Is Yours to Change*, a volume of essays published as a response to the terrorist attacks of September 11, 2001, opens with the following lines embodying the spirit of awareness of our shared humanity:

> To desire peace, to wish for the happiness of one's family, to seek a secure and safe life – these are the shared sentiments of people everywhere. There is no parent anywhere who does not grieve at the death of a child in war (Ikeda 2002, 3).

This vision of a shared humanity emerges with intensified poignancy in "Another Way of Seeing Things," an essay included in the same volume. In a section titled "We Are All Citizens of Earth," Ikeda writes:

> If we think about it, people are not born Turks or Americans. They are not born Palestinian or Jews. These are merely labels. Each of us is born as a precious entity of life, as a human being. Our mothers didn't give birth to us thinking "I'm giving birth to a Japanese" or "I'm giving birth to an Arab." Their only thought was "May this new life be healthy and grow!" (Ibid., 100–1).

It is humanity at that basic level that Ikeda seeks to establish at the center of his dialogues. When he asks his interlocutors to share stories about their childhood, he extends an invitation to reconnect to a kind of innocence, to attain a kind of "cultivated naïveté,"[1] and speak to one another as fellow human beings.

In reading these passages from *The World Is Yours to Change* one perceives a sense of urgency. Ikeda identifies what he calls "obsessions with differences" (Tu and Ikeda 2011, 41) and "[the pursuit] of a continual course of fragmentation" (Ikeda 2010, 165) as the spiritual illness of modern civilization. He goes as far as to claim that "'goodness' can be defined as that which moves us in the direction of harmonious coexistence, empathy and solidarity with others," and that, in contrast, "[t]he nature of evil (…) is to divide: people from people, humanity from the rest of nature" (Ibid., 115). He even describes the effects of this kind of evil in terms of a "pathology of divisiveness" that "drives people to an unreasoning attachment to difference and blinds them to human commonalities" (Ibid.). This pathology, Ikeda claims, "is not limited to individuals but constitutes the deep psychology of collective egoism, which takes its most destructive form in virulent strains of ethnocentrism, and nationalism" (Ibid.). Ikeda's philosophical project is marked by an imperative to promote dialogue and global citizenship.

We can see that the language is intensely morally charged, and that to describe Ikeda's call for "harmonious coexistence, empathy and solidarity" as an "imperative" is no exaggeration. If we consider the first thesis proposed here, that one of the functions of dialogue is to reveal our shared humanity – a thoroughly uncontroversial thesis – we see that, for Ikeda, the stakes for dialogue are very high. We can also understand why he has engaged in what Urbain calls "a whirlwind of dialogue" meeting "more than 7000 scholars, political and opinion leaders from virtually all countries" (Urbain 2010, 137) and why Urbain considers dialogue "as the axis around which the whole system [of Ikeda's philosophy of peace] revolves" (Ibid., 115). However, as essential as the empathetic function of dialogue is, an appraisal of Ikeda's philosophy of dialogue would not be complete without an account of the role of competition.

Dialogue, *agon*, and humanitarian competition

Ikeda appreciates the moral and creative value of dialogue as a method for seeking common ground across differences. At the same time, he also appreciates the value of competition and the creative tensions inherent in growth and learning. Ikeda is very clear and consistent on the principle that common ground must be pursued. However, sooner or later, we all eventually run into differences that for all practical purposes we consider irreconcilable. Even the most experienced in the art of dialogue do.

When describing the creative function of competition Ikeda often speaks of "humanitarian competition," a concept he borrows from Tsunesaburo Makiguchi. Ikeda speaks of Makiguchi's conception of various forms of competition as "a driving force in history" (Ikeda 2010, 6), a view "[i]nfluenced (…) by the Darwinian image of evolution" (Ibid.). In Makiguchi's theory, humanitarian competition represents the peak of an evolutionary process going through "shifts over time in modes of national competition: from the military, to the political, to the economic" (Ibid.). In contrast to the previous modes of competition leading to it, Ikeda explains, humanitarian competition,

> [R]epresents a profound qualitative transformation in the very nature of competition, toward one that is based on a recognition of the interrelatedness and interdependence of human communities and that emphasizes the cooperative aspects of living (…) [Makiguchi] envisaged a time when people and countries would compete – in the original sense of "seeking together" – to make the greatest contribution to human happiness and well-being (Ibid., 6–7).

The kind of competition represented by the concept of "humanitarian competition" is not mutually exclusive with the notions of harmony and collaboration implicit in the idea of empathy explored in the previous section. In fact, the mutual implication of harmony and tension lies at the heart of Ikeda's philosophy of dialogue.

It is interesting that Makiguchi dedicates to the idea of "humanitarian competition" only a brief treatment confined to two pages towards the end of a section in *Geography of Human Life*,[2] but Ikeda, by contrast, returns to "humanitarian competition" time and again. Urbain tells us that, for example, "humanitarian competition" appears as central theme in Ikeda's annual peace proposals 11 times between 1996 and 2009 (Urbain 2010, 152), and again in his 2011 proposal (Ikeda 2011, 17). In the dialogues, for example, the concept appears in *New Horizons in Eastern Humanism*, with Tu Weiming (2011); *Global Civilization*, with Majid Tehranian (2011); *A Quest for Global Peace*, with Joseph Rotblat (2007); *A Passage to Peace*, with Nur Yalman (2008); *Moral Lessons of the Twentieth Century*, with Mikhail Gorbachev (2005), and *A Dialogue Between East and West*, with Ricardo Díez-Hochleitner (2008), amongst others. Ikeda never fails to credit Makiguchi when referring to "humanitarian competition," but in many ways he has made the concept his own.

One sense in which Ikeda appropriates the idea of "humanitarian competition" is especially significant for his philosophy of dialogue. As a Japanese Buddhist who engages in dialogue with Western intellectuals and leaders, Ikeda often finds himself as a representative of a tradition. Since his interlocutors usually provide a perspective based on their own expertise and culture, Ikeda's contributions to a discussion on a topic often come from Buddhism. Over the years, Ikeda has seen how the specific Buddhist outlook he brings to the dialogic exchange can have a transformative effect on his interlocutor, and he has experienced his own interpretation of Buddhism changing over the years through the encounters with other points of view.[3] Because of this, Ikeda has a poignant sense of the value of particular points of view, and can recognize the dangers behind the impulse of pursuing a kind of consensus that erases all differences, well-intentioned as that impulse may be. What Ikeda wants is a mode of dialogic collaboration that preserves differences and allows for competition and tension. He speaks to this effect in his 2011 Peace Proposal where he writes:

> I believe it would be valuable for the world's religions to engage in what the founding president of our organization, Tsunesaburo Makiguchi (1871–1944), termed "humanitarian competition" – that we conduct dialogue toward the shared goal of constructing a culture of human rights and, reflecting on our respective origins and histories, mutually strive to foster in people the capacity to take the lead in this endeavor (Ikeda 2011, 17).

In this passage, Ikeda emphasizes the collaborative aspect of "humanitarian competition," through the vision of "the shared goal of constructing a culture of human rights." In an essay published almost 20 years earlier, he emphasizes

the other side of "humanitarian competition," the preservation of diverse perspectives: "[R]ather than attempt an unprincipled compromise or collusion
among different religions, we should instead encourage them to compete in
the task of producing world citizens" (Ikeda 2010, 187). I would like to suggest that we think of this aspect of humanitarian competition as an *agonistic*
moment.

"Agonistic" refers to competition or rivalry, but it is different from
"antagonistic." The latter carries connotations of hostility, and its fundamental impulse is that of eliminating the enemy. The former, on the other
hand, is rooted in the idea of adversaries, and its fundamental impulse is
that of growing together through competition, or, in Ikeda's words again:
"the original sense of 'seeking together'" (Ibid., 7). The root of the term is
the Classical Greek *agon* (ἀγών), whose literal meaning is "competition"
and is associated with the Olympic Games, an enduring ideal of competitive
camaraderie.[4]

In recent years, interest in the idea of *agon* has been rekindled through
the work of political theorist Chantal Mouffe (2005). My own use of *agon*
to describe an aspect of Ikeda's philosophy of dialogue partakes in meanings
operative in Mouffe's theory of *agonistic pluralism*. I am referring to Mouffe's
critique of what she calls "the typical liberal understanding of pluralism,"
which is that the many perspectives and values working in social life are
reducible to a picture of the world in which the tensions of conflict can be
thoroughly overcome. In her own words:

> The typical liberal understanding of pluralism is that we live in
> a world in which there are indeed many perspectives and values
> and that, owing to empirical limitations, we will never be able to
> adopt them all, but that, when put together, they constitute an
> harmonious and non-conflictual ensemble. This is why this type of
> liberalism must negate the political in its antagonistic dimension
> (Mouffe 2005, 10).

I see in Ikeda an *agonistic* moment in his rejection of any notion of harmony
that implies the erasure of differences. Sharon Todd (2010), commenting on
Mouffe's theory, identifies an important reason for upholding *agonism* when

she asserts that the inevitability of conflict arises "out of holding different viewpoints, subject positions, and identifications, which are always amenable to change over time." For her [Mouffe], the plural nature of social life cannot thereby be 'overcome,' nor should it be" (Todd 2010, 217). This is exactly the reason Ikeda also wants to preserve a diversity of perspectives and maintain a kind of creative tension amongst them: because perspectives "are always amenable to change over time." In subsequent sections I argue for this claim based on the Buddhist conception of the world as interconnected and impermanent.

There is, however, a specific point on which I want to distance my interpretation of Ikeda from Mouffe's theory. For Mouffe, the *agonistic* is opposed to the dialogical, and she identifies the latter as the method associated with the liberal understanding of pluralism against which she stands:

> Adversaries do fight – even fiercely – but according to a shared set of rules, and their positions, despite being ultimately irreconcilable, are accepted as legitimate perspectives. The fundamental difference between the "dialogical" and the "agonistic" perspectives is that the aim of the latter is a profound transformation of the existing power relations and the establishment of a new hegemony (Mouffe 2005, 52).

For Ikeda, as his comments on "humanitarian competition" show, dialogue and competition are not mutually exclusive opposites, but bound up together. An important implication of the *agonistic* function of dialogue is that it must seek a transformation that cannot be primarily "of existing power relations and the establishment of a new hegemony," but a transformation that takes place primarily at the levels of the self and values, and only derivatively at the level of power relations.

Having established the connections between humanitarian competition and dialogue, and having clarified the meaning of the *agonistic* function of dialogue, let us consider a few examples of how Ikeda deals with conflict and tension in the published dialogues. Urbain (2010) addresses this question. He quotes from *Choose Life*, the Ikeda–Toynbee dialogue, and highlights how Ikeda deals with disagreement on the issues of mitigating greed, the moral status of homosexuality, euthanasia, and suicide (Urbain 2010, 133–36). Urbain focuses on what he calls the strategy of "using even a disagreement as the starting point to finding common ground" (Ibid., 128). Here, however, I want to suggest that we look at moments of tension and disagreement in Ikeda not only as "starting points to finding common ground," but also as genuinely *agonistic* moments.

On the issue of suicide, for example, Ikeda and Toynbee disagree, and it does not seem to be the case that they are able to reach further common ground *from* this disagreement. Rather, perhaps because of a foundation of mutual respect and trust, they are able to further pursue an enriching exchange *despite* their differences. But the fact of the disagreement remains, I believe, as a point of tension. Toynbee insists that in some cases "suicide is legitimate and to put obstacles in the way of it is very wrong" (Toynbee and Ikeda 2008, 165). He refers to the cases of an artist and a writer who, because of misfortunes, became incapable of using their talents and consequently lost their source of meaning in life. Ikeda responds that "[t]alent and the ability to reason are only a part, not all, of the total entity of life," and that "[t]o argue that once a person's abilities have failed, he can no longer live in a meaningful way is to put too narrow an interpretation on life itself" (Ibid., 165). Toynbee finds suicide morally permissible in some cases; Ikeda finds it condemnable without exception. Their respective positions are directly related to beliefs central to their convictions: for Toynbee it is the very sense of meaning in life that comes from a humanistic conception of dignity associated with the fruits of reason, creativity and labor; for Ikeda, it is the sense of meaning derived from the Buddhist concept of life force, which is inherent in all life. For both of them, these are convictions they simply cannot compromise, and they realize that the disagreement is too fundamental to be bridged by exercises of linguistic and cultural translation.[5]

Irreconcilable differences can be sources of great value, provided that they do not hurt the relationship. The humanistic moral vision at which Ikeda and Toynbee arrive cooperatively through dialogue is enriched, not compromised, by the fact of their irreconcilable differences. That these differences remain despite their tenacious efforts in pursuit of common ground is in itself a hopeful message. The challenge of dialogue and cooperation might seem daunting for people standing across the divide of differences perceived as irreconcilable. But the fact that dialogue can lead to cooperation and value creation *despite* irreconcilable, or at least not-yet-reconciled, differences is a source of hope for those who perceive themselves as being in a similar position.

Another example of vigorous disagreement in the published dialogues appears in *Before it is Too Late*, with Aurelio Peccei, founder of the Club of Rome. It includes an interesting passage where Ikeda explicitly articulates reasons for refusing to pursue agreement. I quote at length:

> **Peccei:** *Have the different religions risen to the challenge of this epochal crisis?* (...) Have all these great religions [Buddhism, Christianity, Islam] ever called on the other major faiths to work and learn together how to guide the world population away from its present plight and towards terrestrial salvation before it is too late? (...) Though diverging not so much on the essence of the good as on its revelation, formulation or interpretation, will religions remain incapable of converging in a superior vision of what combining their unparalleled spiritual and moral forces could do to make humanity better and thus to open roads to a future reality worth living? (...) [C]an the great inspiration of ecumenism be brought to the practical expression of religious accord, solidarity and cooperation in the pursuance of the good of all men?

> **Ikeda:** The questions you ask are stern ones demanding honest and serious thought. To be perfectly frank, I consider the ecumenical movement being sponsored by a number of religions today nothing short of deception. Any religion, to remain a religion, must be convinced that its own doctrines are uniquely correct and that other doctrines are mistaken. In actual practice ecumenism would demand compromise on doctrinal matters that I consider unacceptable (...) I believe that cooperation among religious bodies, though impossible on the plane of doctrine and teaching, is not only possible, but also essential, on the quite different planes of politics, economy, industry and culture (Peccei and Ikeda 1984, 97–8).

For Peccei, practical collaboration is not enough; he wants to pursue consensus-building all the way down to the roots of morality, "converging in a superior vision of what combining their unparalleled spiritual and moral

forces could do." This is, by the way, a case of "the typical liberal understanding of pluralism" that Mouffe attacks, if not a kind of monism that
Mouffe would find even more implausible. Ikeda, on the other hand, wants
to preserve diversity, both because he wants to maintain the right to hold the
conviction that beliefs can be "uniquely correct," and because he understands
that it is from diversity that the creative forces of humanitarian competition
can be unleashed.

As I have been trying to argue, enduring differences need not be an obstacle
for value creation through dialogue. The work of dialogue does not require a
telos of complete agreement. Complete agreement in all significant aspects is
not only impossible, but from a cosmopolitan perspective it is also undesir-
able. Shared values and understanding bring about the obvious intrinsic value
of empathy and the clear instrumental value of enabling collaboration. At the
same time, shared values and understanding also embody a special kind of
instrumental value: that of allowing for insurmountable difference to exist in
creative rather than destructive tension: to be *agonistic* rather than *antagonistic*.

An interconnected, impermanent world

For Ikeda genuine dialogue entails an engagement with the complexity and
unfathomability of life through the encounter with another individual. In
this sense, dialogue, like life, qualifies as a case of what he calls "complex
and intangible phenomena" (Ikeda 1982, 49), of which "in Buddhist philosophy (...) it is not considered possible to reach an understanding (...) by
examining them from a single fixed viewpoint" (Ibid.). Often, in the face of a
phenomenon that defies precise description from "a single fixed viewpoint,"
we suggest a space of tension between clearly articulable perspectives. It is
my contention that for Ikeda dialogue is an artful practice that takes place in
the space of tension between empathy and *agon*. Dialogue is a phenomenon
towards which "one must be flexible and adopt a number of viewpoints"
(Ibid., 49). The multiple viewpoints to which Ikeda makes reference here
are articulated in the Buddhist principle of *the three perceptions*, which provides a picture of the world grounded in an ontology of interconnectedness
and impermanence.

The theory of *the three perceptions* was originally developed by the founder
of the T'ien-T'ai school of Mahayana Buddhism, Chih-i (538–96).[6] Chih-i

is a towering figure in Chinese Buddhism, and the doctrines of the T'ien-T'ai school (Tendai, in Japanese) constitute the religious and philosophical foundation for much of the developments in Buddhist thought in medieval Japan.[7] Through his teaching of the *three perceptions*, Chih-i expanded the traditional Madhyamika (Middle Way) doctrine of the *two truths* – "mundane worldly truth" and "supreme truth"[8] – into what sometimes is translated as "provisional perception" (Jp. *ketai*), "perception of the latent" (Jp. *kūtai*), and "perception of the middle way" (Jp. *chūtai*). In this section I introduce Ikeda's interpretation of *the three perceptions* and make a case for its significance in his philosophy of dialogue.

Provisional perception (*ketai*)

When we look at the world from the perspective of provisional perception, or *ketai*, we regard things in their conventional, temporary nature, what Nagarjuna (*ca*. 150–250), founder of the Madhyamika tradition, calls "mundane worldly truth." Candrakirti (*ca*. 560–640), for example, described it as "like a covering of ignorance which obscures the true nature of reality" and as "consist[ing] of that which is conceptualized and understood through the medium of language and discriminative, cognitive thought" (Swanson 1989, 2). Even though "supreme truth" lies beyond the realm of language and conceptualization, there is a sense in which words and concepts when employed with skill can be "expedient means," which point to the truth and lead to it. Provisional perception is the perspective of the world represented through words and concepts. It does not capture the nature of reality but it can be employed as an expedient means to reveal truths that lie beyond concepts.

The conceptual representation of the world provided by *ketai* reveals things in the actuality of their physical existence. Ikeda writes, "appearance, which is equated with Provisional Perception means all things we can detect with our senses (...) and I include in this minute particles and the like, which we can see only with electron microscopes, as well as invisible phenomena such as sound waves" (Ikeda 1982, 51). To put it simply, *ke* in *ketai* refers to the physical world.[9]

The character *ke*, in *ketai* can be translated as "the provisional," "temporary existence," or "impermanence." Buddhism characterizes physical phenomena with an emphasis on the dynamic and transitory nature of reality: "In

Buddhist thinking, all these things are temporary or transitory, and they are constantly undergoing change, being brought together or dispersed by causes and conditions" (Ibid.). Our lives, as they are grounded in the physicality of the human body, also exist in a state of constant change: "Buddhism emphasizes the continuous change going on in human life, pointing out that our perceptible lives on earth are constantly undergoing birth, maturation, destruction, and latency (...) 'all is in flux and there is no permanence'" (Ibid.). The impermanence of the world is ubiquitous: "the more deeply we go into the physical aspects of the cosmos, the more convincing the evidence of unceasing change and flux everywhere" (Ibid., 53).

Swanson (1989, 5) clarifies the connection between "conventional" and "temporary existence": "Our phenomenal world has temporary reality in the sense of an integrated, co-arising, interdependent relationship of causes and conditions. This is called 'conventional' existence." When we regard the world through conceptual representation, we see things in their actuality, which Buddhism regards as defined by impermanence. The moral import of this insistence on the impermanence of all things is the idea that we cannot escape this condition. Ikeda raises the normative question about imperman-ence, "how do we cope with the world around us? Do we flee from it? Do we challenge it?" (Ikeda 1982, 51), and immediately answers: "Fleeing does not accord with Buddhism, for it implies that the truth of impermanence is somehow repugnant" (Ibid.). "Actually," he adds, "the realization of the constantly changing nature of all things is the key to true happiness, for it means that no matter how bad a situation is, it will change. No misfortune is permanent; no evil insuperable" (Ibid.). From this perspective, happiness is constitutive of the wisdom to understand this principle of impermanence; such understanding entails the capacity to respond to it creatively.

Perception of the latent (*kūtai*)

The other side of *ke* is *kū*. In the Madhyamika tradition, it is often called "emptiness," "nothingness," "Void," "non-substantiality," or, in the original Sanskrit, "*śūnyatā*." In *Life: An Enigma, a Precious Jewel*, Ikeda describes *kū* as "the nature and spirit of all things – what is sometimes called *noumenon*" (Ikeda 1982, 54). Perhaps concerned about inviting the usual mistake of equating "spirit" with the notion of "soul," Ikeda adds, "*Kū* is not simply the spirit of human beings. It is the character and essence of all things." For example, diamond and coal are both made of carbon atoms, but their molecular structures make them drastically different. "*Kū*," Ikeda explains, "is the fundamental nature making diamonds diamonds and coal coal" (Ibid., 55). The nature of diamond and coal lies in the internal relations of their molecular structures. Similarly, our biological endowments are composed of the same basic elements, but the complexity of each individual life makes each of us unique and different.

Individuality comes from the complexity of relations *internal* and *external* to a thing. What makes water what it is and not something else is, in part, the way water relates to other things in the world, like the fact that it does not mix with oil, that it relates to our vision by means of certain qualities of transparency and fluidity, and that it relates to the human body by quenching thirst. In this sense, *kū* refers to potentiality.

Ikeda writes: "Perhaps the best way to understand this interpretation [of *kū* as potentiality] is to consider that nothing exists except in relation to everything else, which is to say, the totality of the cosmos" (Ibid., 26). The latent potential of an individual resides in unrealized interactions with its surroundings. John Dewey, for example, develops a concept of potential as possibility of transactions that is very similar to what I propose here as an interpretation of potentiality in Ikeda.[10] For Buddhism, it is this aspect of potentiality that constitutes what we understand as the nature of a thing.

The Middle Way (*chūtai*)

One sense of the Middle Way refers to walking a path avoiding extremes. The extremes from which the Middle Way steers clear are, in Swanson's words, "the affirmation of substantial Being on the one hand ('eternalism'), and nihilistic denial of all existence on the other ('annihilationism')" (Swanson 1989, 5). In this sense, the middle way embodies the recognition of provisional perception and perception of the latent as containing aspects of truth, and that moral wisdom entails holding these truths simultaneously. This moral middle ground between extremes resembles the Aristotelian idea of virtue, and the Confucian notion of ethical middle way. There is, however, another dimension to the concept of *chū*, articulated in Ikeda's ontological interpretation of *chū* as essential self.[11]

Ikeda writes that *chū* is "the essential entity of life, which supports the physical aspect and the spiritual aspect, *ke* and *kū,* and contains them both" (Ikeda 1982, 61). The "essential entity of life" is *chū* as an ontology of the self, in Ikeda's words: *"essential self"* (Ibid.). According to Ikeda, there is an "enduring self" (Ikeda 1996, 119–27) underlying the all-pervasive impermanence and non-substantiality of being. He refers to it as a "continuum, [that] preserves (…) individual being" (Ikeda 1982, 61), and as an "unchanging reality," that makes an individual himself and "keeps him from becoming [someone else]" (Ibid.).

Ikeda's language, with words like "essential entity," "essential self," and "unchanging reality" can be misconstrued as positing a transcendent, substantial Being of the kind that the concept of *kū* is supposed to deny. However, Ikeda is quick to point out that the three perceptions are "one reality viewed from three different standpoints, not three separate entities" (Ibid., 63). There is no such thing as an "essential self" or an "unchanging reality" as an ontologically separate entity. "The middle way sustains the tangible and the intangible, *ke* and *kū*, but that is not the whole story of the nature of life. The middle way appears in the tangible, and it exists in the *kū*" (Ibid.). The continuum of self that is *chū* exists fully integrated with the impermanence and the non-substantiality of life. That is the point that Chih-i makes in *The Profound Meaning of the Lotus Sutra* (Ch. *Fa hua hsüan i*), when he states that "This threefold truth is perfectly integrated; one-in-three and three-in-one" (Swanson 1989, 7). In concurrence with Ikeda's interpretation, Swanson reminds us that *chū*, in its integration with *ke* and *kū*, must not be understood as transcendent, but that the middle way is "manifested in and through and is identical with temporal phenomenal reality, which is again in turn empty of an unchanging substance" (Ibid., 6).

What Ikeda tries to do with his interpretation of the middle way as an *essential self*, I believe, is to preserve the notion of a moral center for the self in a world where everything is changing and all life is interconnected. At the same time, by interpreting *chū* as an "unchanging reality" Ikeda emphasizes the sense in which life is relatively stable and harmonious, and *that* is what he calls the *essential self*. I believe the key to understanding this notion of *essential self* is in the distinction between what Buddhism calls the "lesser self" and the "greater self." The "'lesser self,'" Ikeda writes, is a self "caught up in the snares of egoism," while "the 'greater self,' [is] fused with the life of the universe" (Ikeda 1996, 161). *Chū* as *essential self* is the *greater self*, which is identified with the totality of life. "What is this larger [greater] self?" Ikeda ponders in an essay titled "The Enduring Self," "It is the basic principle of the whole universe" (Ibid., 123). While everything in the universe exists as impermanent and interdependent, the totality of life as such is stable and harmonious, not by means of transcending impermanence and interdependence, but through it. The reason why Ikeda claims that the "unification of the three truths (...) transcends verbal expression" (Ibid., 93) is that it refers to the life of the universe as a whole, and there is no such thing as standing outside of it to take the necessary distance for conceptual and linguistic articulation. For Ikeda, understanding of the reality of life is one with the attainment of the *greater self* as "the openness and expansiveness of character that embraces the suffering of all people as one's own" (Ibid., 162). In other words, understanding of the nature of reality is not achieved by means of detached contemplation, but by means of compassionate engagement.

Three aspects of dialogue

The implications of the doctrine of the three perceptions for a philosophy of dialogue are wide ranging. In this chapter I cannot explore them all, but I propose three aspects of dialogue in Ikeda that I identify as connected with *ke*, *kū*, and *chū*. They are "Dialogue as Work of Persistence," "Dialogue Beyond Concepts," and "Dialogue as Artful Practice." I conclude with some remarks on the nature of the moral ideal of the greater self.

Dialogue as work of persistence

In the Buddhist principle of impermanence Ikeda finds a source of hope. Suffering comes from clinging to the illusion of permanence: "everything shifts from instant to instant like the current of a mighty river (...) clinging fast to the illusion of permanence causes the sufferings of the human spirit" (Ikeda 1996, 121). Conversely, happiness comes from the realization of impermanence as a source of hope, as Ikeda wrote in a passage mentioned earlier: "the realization of the constantly changing nature of all things is the key to true happiness, for it means that no matter how bad a situation is, it will change. No misfortune is permanent, no evil insuperable" (Ikeda 1982, 51). The fact that everything is bound to change is a reason to reject defeatism and despair in the face of seemingly intractable conflict.

Ikeda gives poetic articulation to the idea of persistence in dialogue:

> Dialogue is also, in a way, painstaking work. It may not always lead to immediate solutions, but it stimulates the mind and the spirit in ways that tap into the source of human wisdom. Repeated dialogue points out the path humanity needs to travel (Bosco et. al. 2009, 3).

This view of impermanence as a call for persistence and hope is one of the central principles of Ikeda's philosophy of dialogue.

Temporary existence, *ke*, is a double-sided concept. On the one hand, it refers to impermanence. On the other hand, it refers to actuality: *ke* means *temporary* existence, and it also means temporary *existence*. Even when values and traditions are temporary, they exist, and they matter. As we persist in the path of dialogue, we must attend to the demands of our commitments and traditions, for they provide relative stability to our normative lives. Such relative stability is a requirement for creative engagement.

When Ikeda writes that, "for all its impermanence, life is magnificently harmonious" (Ikeda 1982, 53), we can intuitively agree. But we can also resonate with the converse: that for all its harmony, life is direfully impermanent. This is because "clinging fast to the illusion of permanence" not only, as Ikeda reminds us, "causes the sufferings of the human spirit" (Ikeda 1996, 121), but is also very natural, very human. We need relative stability, and a robust philosophy of dialogue must account for this need. The sense of hope for the possibility of change that Ikeda derives from recognition of the impermanence of all things must be balanced with the possibility of bringing about relative stability through dialogue or in dialogue. We patiently persist in the work of dialogue because value creative change come s about gradually.

Dialogue beyond concepts

Ikeda describes *kū* as exceptionally difficult to explain because "*kū* defies positive description" (Ikeda 1982, 56) and it refers to "the idea of breaking through the traditional distinction between existence and non-existence" (Ibid., 60). *Kū* expresses an aspect of reality that lies beyond the conceptual. Ikeda reminds us that this non-conceptual reality permeates all of existence: "the essence of the cosmos itself can be regarded as being in the state of *kū*" (Ibid.). If this is true, the implications of developing, or failing to develop, adequate modes of understanding and communication that go beyond the conceptual are great.

Commenting on Chih-i's philosophical system, Ikeda notes: "[it] represents an attempt to explain the mutually inclusive relationship of the ultimate truth and the phenomenal world, of the absolute and the relative" (Ikeda 1986, 119). For Ikeda, the universal and the particular are mutually inclusive, and anything more determinate that could be said about their relationship would simply be inadequate.[12] This is because, in Ikeda's own words, "true understanding lies on a level that transcends verbal expression" (Ibid., 93) and, paraphrasing a Buddhist saying, "enlightenment lies at the place 'where words and phrases are cut off and the actions of the mind come to an end'" (Ibid.).

Before action, reality is creative potential through and through; it exists in the state of *kū*. It is action that determines reality into a particular manifestation by means of actualizing one of many possibilities. "Action" and "actual" share etymological roots. Potentially, before action, we uphold both universal and particular loyalties at once. In the moment of action we must choose. Moral systems provide some degree of guidance on how to make choices between conflicting values, but part of being a cosmopolitan is to leave some room to reject full determination of action by moral systems. Because we value valuing and we value critical perspectives, because we value creativity with respect to values, we want to leave questions of value to be finally determined at the moment of action, at the moment of actualization.[13] In this sense, both local and universal values are what Hansen describes as "provisional and emergent from human interaction and dialogue, rather than asserted as a metaphysical foundation" (Hansen 2010b, 2). In fact, from the perspective of the principle of *kū*, values are metaphysically provisional and emergent.

The task of cosmopolitan dialogue entails both a constant rediscovery of our cultural and moral roots and the charting of new normative terrains. This double gesture is expressed in the phrase "Socratic world citizens," which Ikeda uses to describe his vision of cosmopolitans steeped in the art of "[e]ducation, based on dialogue (...) [that] enables us to rise above the confines of our parochial perspectives and passions" and who are leaders in "the search for new principles for the peaceful integration of the world" (Ikeda 1996, 173–74). Ikeda's vision is that as a result of widely spreading the practice of persistent dialogue, we come to advance "the process of shaping the kind of global ethic that must undergird global citizenship" (Ikeda 2010, 119). A philosophy of dialogue grounded in the principle of *kū* regards that all values, particular and universal, traditional and new, are provisional and emergent, and that the art of dialogue is the art of value creation.

Dialogue as artful practice

Earlier, I mentioned Swanson's useful account of the Middle Way as a virtuous middle path between the extremes of "eternalism" and "annihilationism" (Swanson 1989, 5). Avoiding eternalism entails that dialogue cannot be conceived as shared pursuit of a pre-established, unchanging truth. Dialogue must be attuned to the ever-changing, full of latent potential nature of reality. From the perspective of avoiding eternalism, persistence in the work of dialogue is not directed towards the attainment of pre-established values, but towards the possibility of value creation. On the other hand, steering clear from annihilationism entails that there are aspects of reality that matter to all or some of us, and that our attitude in dialogue should not be only about creating *new* values from the encounter, but also preserving values, re-creating values. This vision of dialogue as a practice of steering a middle course between extremes suggests that, for Ikeda, wisdom in dialogue cannot be reduced to a set of rules. There is no algorithm of genuine dialogue; instead, we should think of dialogue as an artful practice.

The path of dialogue runs in the delicate balance between change and persistence, and this requires a particular sensibility. When attempting to convince others to adopt our values and practices, we must do it empathetically, understanding their values, and respecting them. When opening our values to change, we must offer some resistance; we must embody some sense of moral and cultural grounding from which to judge others' values. It is through the interplay of these two functions, empathy and *agon*, that in dialogue we come to achieve harmonious stability of values in tension and come to create new values in the encounter with difference. The idea of the greater self, as moral character to openly embrace all of life, does not mean to lose one's individuality for the sake of collective good. Rather, it means to engage the sufferings and joys of others, to engage the normative demands of the world in creative tension with one's own desires and values.

The moral ideal of the Greater Self

The nature of reality for Ikeda is one that allows for what Urbain (2010) calls "inner transformation," but an inner transformation that is never permanent and that is not separate from the interconnectedness of the world: it must be conquered anew constantly and it must do so in engagement with the world through compassionate relationships with others. In other words, the Buddhist ontology developed here rejects a picture of inner transformation based on the metaphor of transcendence onto an ontologically separate plane of existence. Instead, it presents a picture of moral wisdom as grounded in the dynamics of life in the world and responsive to changes in the environment.[14]

For Ikeda, dialogue must be an aspect of any valid moral life because unclouded moral perception necessitates dialogue:

> Reality can be revealed only through genuine dialogue, where "self"
> and "other" transcend the narrow limits of ego and fully interact.
> This inclusive sense of reality expresses a human spirituality
> abounding in vitality and empathy (Ikeda 2010, 56).

When "'self' and 'other' transcend the narrow limits of ego" the self is not really perceived as separate from the environment, hence the quotation marks around "self" and "other." The world of impermanence and interconnectedness can be a source of "vitality and empathy" when perceived from the perspective of the oneness of self and environment. On the other hand, if we regard the

self as an entity separate from the environment, if we see the self as an individual consciousness in an individual body, concerned with itself, pursuing
only its own security, well-being and pleasure, then interconnectedness and
impermanence are serious problems. Impermanence inevitably brings about
the end of *this* self and its precious goods. Interconnectedness acquires the
aspect of constraints and the burden of dependence.

When such vision of the self is asserted metaphysically as essential human
nature or, less strongly, as part of evolutionarily determined human nature,
the response is to avoid the problems of impermanence and interconnectedness by limiting the scope and depth of these phenomena. These efforts are,
naturally, bound to work only temporarily and ultimately are bound to fail.
The only consolation for such a vision of human nature is transcendence onto
a supernatural realm of purity and eternity. Buddhism recognizes this kind
of self but it asserts it much less strongly: as a tendency. It also recognizes its
counterpart, also attainable within the means of our constrained nature: the
greater self.

As I state in the introduction to this chapter, it is my contention that the
heart of Ikeda's philosophy of dialogue resides in the moral ideal of the greater
self. The concept of *chū*, or middle way, in its two senses of moral center
and essential self, is very close to the idea of the greater self. It is possible
that in Ikeda they are interchangeable, but it would be the task of a separate
study to determine that. What we can confidently observe, however, is that
Ikeda's descriptions of the greater self resemble those of *chū*: sometimes they
stay close to the everyday, speaking of caring for a single individual in direct
encounter, sometimes they soar to heights approaching the esoteric, speaking
of compassionately embracing the totality of life. Just as with *chū*, there is no
sense of supernatural transcendence in the idea of the greater self. It basically
comes down to a moral discipline that integrates the particular, caring for a
single individual, with the universal, the totality of life.

The vision of cosmopolitan dialogue that I propose here is at the heart of
the moral discipline of the greater self. It consists of this: in the encounter
with the other, we recognize someone genuinely different, and whether
the other is a family member or someone from a foreign culture it is only a
matter of degree. In this difference a tension arises, which we inhabit through
empathy and *agon*. Here the first moment of the discipline of the greater self

comes into play: *the courage not to fear difference*. If we muster the courage to genuinely enter into dialogue across difference, we begin to recognize in the other an individual life. Here comes the second moment: *compassion to feel empathy*. And as we do this, the third moment of the discipline of the greater self takes place: the *recognition* that just as we share this empathetic connection so *is all life interconnected*. This is the life condition of the greater self. It is a discipline cultivated in concrete encounters. In Ikeda's words, the greater self "always seeks ways of alleviating the pain, and augmenting the happiness, of others, *here, amid the realities of everyday life*" (Ikeda 1996, 162). The greater self is not a prerequisite for dialogue, but it is a constantly emerging moral ideal cultivated through dialogue. It is what Ikeda elsewhere describes as "the global citizen" (see above). Rather than the esoteric images that some of the language might evoke, the greater self captures a sense of reverence inherent in everyday encounters.

Conclusion

For Ikeda, the spirit of cosmopolitanism has deeply personal roots. As a teenager, he saw the militaristic nationalism of Japan bring the nation to ruin and cause tragedy to his family and community.[15] Even before he encountered the teachings of Buddhism, he was in search of a philosophy that could transcend the narrow-mindedness of nationalism. In Buddhism, Ikeda found such a philosophy through the principle of the three perceptions, which postulates the interdependence of all life and upholding human dignity irrespective of nationality, religion, ethnicity or cultural background. But it was not by principle that Ikeda adopted Buddhism. Rather, it was the moral character of an individual, Josei Toda, that inspired young Ikeda to embrace Buddhism and dedicate his life to work for peace and walk the path of dialogue.

What Mahayana Buddhism calls the greater self is for Ikeda an account of the life condition that, as a young man, he identified in the moral integrity of his teacher Toda. A life condition, I believe, he recognizes time and again in people of all backgrounds he meets in dialogue. Ikeda's conviction is that dialogue amongst individuals pursuing this ideal is "the path humanity must walk" and constitutes the most secure foundation for peace. In a world thoroughly interconnected and always changing, where people both pursue common ground and compete with one another, the heart of Ikeda's philosophy of dialogue resides in the discipline to exercise the greater self in the encounter with the other. And through this discipline, in turn, recognizing the greater self in the other.

CHAPTER 4

Youth Perspectives: A Case Study of the Application in Australia of Group Dialogues for Peace

Elizabeth Bowen

Introduction

Daisaku Ikeda has set an impressive example of what is possible based on living a life fully engaged and devoted to dialogue. Grappling topics that span cross-cultural, environmental, multi-faith, artistic and spiritual issues and the many impediments to global peace with his dialogue partners, his aim is encapsulated in an interview with Clark Strand: "While staying true to its essence, Buddhism needs to encounter, learn and evolve. In this sense, I am convinced that the work of rediscovery, purification, and universalization – taken on by the SGI as its core mission – is the very essence of Buddhism" (Ikeda in Strand 2008, 3). Ikeda is one of the pioneers in these efforts to encounter different philosophies, cultures and religions, learn from "the other" and develop the expression of Buddhist practice to one relevant to contemporary society. This has been driven by an unerring belief in the power of dialogue and an emphasis on humanism.

Moreover, Ikeda's leadership of Soka Gakkai International, one of his most important legacies, has encouraged social contribution at the local community level by members in over 192 countries and territories. Crucially, how Ikeda's legacy will come to be valued may be largely determined by current and future generations of SGI members. In this respect, many young members of SGI Australia, who may have resisted formalized religion, have embraced a style of "postreligious" practice centered on Ikeda's call for dialogue and emphasis on humanism. By applying the example of Ikeda in creative efforts at dialogue for peace, young people, inspired by this approach to peace, provide a hopeful glimmer of the potential of dialogue as a realistic, rather than merely idealistic, methodology of peace.

This chapter will examine the Australian context of SGI and how young people are engaged in activities that are centered on applying Ikeda's principles of dialogue. It is a case study of how Ikeda's example of employing dialogue as the ultimate strategy for peace is enacted, drawing on the following examples: firstly, the implementation of the group discussion meetings and its impact on youth involvement and secondly, a project where SGI youth have an exchange with Muslim youth. Both these are posed as "postreligious possibilities" where emphasis is placed on interaction, engagement and dialogue. This emphasis differs from a tendency of organizations to focus on theoretical learning internally and on critical comparison of faith traditions in a multi-faith setting. Rather, it is the value of the exchange itself, without specified or imposed outcomes, that fulfills Ikeda's hope that the "practice of humanism is founded on heartfelt, one-to-one dialogue" (Ikeda 2005, 3). This spirit is encapsulated in Martin Buber's words, "All actual life is encounter" (quoted in Ikeda 2005, 9). This approach to dialogue is one that diminishes the import of differences of civilizations and religious traditions, and separation of self and other. It seeks the commonality of the shared struggle of humanity.

Dialogue as a philosophical tradition

Olivier Urbain (2010) proposed in his systemization of Ikeda's philosophy of peace that the promotion of dialogue is one of Ikeda's most pronounced contributions to creating a global culture of peace. He formulates Ikeda's belief and confidence in dialogue as one of the three significant themes characterizing an immense body of work – the other two being inner transformation and global citizenship. Dialogue is central to the triad as it is in pursuing dialogue that opportunities for inner transformation arise and global citizenship is enacted. Urbain examines Ikeda's peace proposals where Ikeda has drawn on classical and modern scholars, including Socrates, Michel de Montaigne and Buber to give theoretical substance to the argument that dialogue is the most creative and hopeful expression of humanity. Ikeda writes of a hatred of language (*misologos* of Socrates), the imposition of a foregone conclusion (Montaigne, "The Art of Conversation") and monologue (the I–it relationship of Buber) as impediments to the humanistic pursuit of dialogue. Fanaticism, dogmatism and self-righteousness are the enemies of dialogue in Ikeda's view. Dialogue or use of language in conversation is the means to encourage and inspire in an open-ended manner, and empathetic listening allows for the true flourishing of dialogue. In 2002, in response to the events of 9/11 and its aftermath, Ikeda poignantly expressed concern over the abandonment of this spirit of dialogue:

> Without dialogue, humans are fated to walk in the darkness of their own dogmatic self-righteousness. Dialogue is the lamp by which we dispel that darkness, lighting and making visible for each other our steps and the path ahead (Ikeda 2002, 30).

The significance of dialogue, Ikeda emphasizes, is that it is the subtle movement of humanism, creating imperceptible ripples and providing gentle resistance to a tidal wave of bureaucracy, ideological conflict and institutional deadlock. It is a slower, deeper movement of history, in Arnold Toynbee's words. Ikeda refers to his dialogue with Toynbee in his (2000) Peace Proposal writing that, "We must confront the reality that there is a deepening crisis of identity that afflicts people everywhere and is driven by what Toynbee termed the 'deeper, slower movements of history' which are not amenable to remedy through purely political means" (Ikeda 2000, 16). Ikeda goes on to say that "It is on this profound level that a paradigm shift toward an intercultural perspective is called for" (Ibid.). In a similar vein, Ikeda uses the analogy of trim tabs – small adjustable flaps on the wings of airplanes and the keels of boats that facilitate the movement of a rudder even on a massive ship or plane. When it comes to efforts at dialogue on the global stage, he writes, humanism operates in the same way as trim tabs (Ikeda 2005, 4). The path of pursuing dialogue, as the surest methodology and tool for peace, may seem painstakingly slow in a "microwave" society in which outcome-driven results are desired instantaneously.

In addition, Urbain (2010) and Majid Tehranian (2003) have linked Ikeda's dialogical methodology with Jürgen Habermas's communicative rationality. As Urbain paraphrases:

> According to Habermas, the public sphere is under constant threat of being colonized by the administrative system. Communicative action theory can be used to protect society against dehumanization, to protect the public sphere against the inhumane struggle for power that often characterizes the administrative sphere (Urbain 2010, 121).

Tehranian summarizes as follows:

> Unlike these two types of rationality [practical and instrumental], critical rationality begins with certain normative ideals with which we compare, contrast and criticize existing conditions. All moral and ideological schools thus participate in the exercise of this kind of rationality by criticizing their worlds from the perspective of their ideal world.

> Habermas's communicative rationality, by contrast, does not begin with ideal constructs except for one that he calls "ideal speech community," characterized by the absence of force and the presence of equality in communicative access and competence of all participants in dialogue (Ikeda and Tehranian 2003, 91).

Although Tehranian goes on to say that such an "ideal speech community" does not exist in reality, it is a useful way of understanding Ikeda's persistence in promoting dialogue and human diplomacy as ways of challenging the "isms" – in particular fanaticism and dogmatism. The group discussion meetings discussed further on could, however, be said to be a close approximation of such a community.

David Bohm (2004) also provides valuable insights into dialogue, which can be useful in examining Ikeda's contribution to the philosophical tradition of dialogue as a pathway to peace. As Bohm writes: "People say, 'All we really need is love.' If there were universal love, all would go well. But we don't appear to have it. So we have to find a way that works." For Bohm this is to reflect on the way in which dialogue can go beyond "cozy adjustment" (Bohm 2004, 15). This is conversation that is comfortable, polite and never goes beyond a surface exchange. Bohm argues for dialogue where assumptions are suspended so they can be examined and opinions can be tested. He talks of creating an empty space that does not have to be filled with decision-making, winning an argument or achieving an agenda. Rather, as he states, "We are not trying to accumulate anything. That's one point about dialogue. As Krishnamurti used to say, 'The cup has to be empty to hold something'" (Ibid., 19). Bohm sees possibilities in "agendaless" dialogues, which allow for a space where collective thought can be nurtured and social coherence based on shared meanings can blossom. As with Ikeda, Bohm believes that this needs to start at the grassroots level. The development of "participatory thought" that forms the foundation for dialogue, Bohm acknowledges, has some dangers, such as being associated with tribalism, and is muddled with literal thought. However, Bohm sees it as a gateway to the unlimited, "not just the direction of going to greater and greater distances out to the end of the universe; but much more importantly, it is also going into more and more subtlety" (Ibid., 107). Ikeda has proven to be a master of such forms of dialogue and it is this style of dialogue that SGI aspires to enact. A significant commonality between Bohm and Ikeda can be gleaned in the conclusion of Bohm's work:

> I think then, that there is the possibility of the transformation of
> consciousness, both individually and collectively. It's important that
> it happens together – it's got to be both. And therefore this whole
> question – of communication and the ability to dialogue, the ability
> to participate in communication – is crucial (Ibid., 109).

It is the transformation of consciousness or, in Ikeda's words, human revolution or inner transformation that is possible in pursuing dialogue in its truest sense. And it is only with such transformation that creative solutions can emerge and humanity can realize the possibilities that Bohm sees as being destroyed by "some rather trivial things" (Ibid., 108).

An evolution in dialogue – Ikeda's self-mastery and risk

A further theme of Ikeda's promotion of dialogue is that of character development, self-mastery, inner transformation and discovering what it is to be truly human through engagement with the other. In his 2005 Peace Proposal Ikeda expresses concern at this age of "free individuals" no longer tied to traditional family and educational institutions and of a "painless civilization" in which people "avoid suffering and pursue pleasure." Face-to-face dialogue in this sense is a confrontation with our humanity and our identity as expressed in the concept "I interact, therefore I am;" an updated interpretation of Descartes' "I think, therefore I am."

One's identity is meaningfully revealed in our expression in the community, and in his 2004 Peace Proposal Ikeda forewarns of the dangers of "virtual disconnection." Prophetically, prior to the widespread use of social networking he warned that virtual communication does not provide the same opportunity to confront or master our self at any depth. He wrote: "Virtual reality is fundamentally incompatible with an uncomfortable, even painful – yet essential – aspect of human experience; the way our encounters with others force us to face and confront ourselves, and the inner struggle that this sparks" (Ikeda 2004, 25).

From this perspective, new forms of social networking that provide endless opportunities to connect with others do not provide this same opportunity for self-mastery, development of character and empathy for the other that underpins heartfelt, one-to-one dialogue. Twitter, Facebook and SMS are communication tools many young people are adeptly familiar with. They form part of a phenomenon that has changed the landscape of information and communication technologies as well as how relationships are formed and sustained. While these technologies make possible communication across the globe, and teenagers are able to "Facebook" their friends from their bedroom, whether this type of communication provides enriching encounters of self and other, or in Buber's words the "I–You" as opposed to an "I–it" relationship is yet to be seen. It is the development of character – elements of which are wisdom, compassion and self-mastery to engage in this kind of dialogue – that Ikeda wishes to inspire through his example.

Ikeda also poses dialogue as a risk. Drawing on Buber's work, he writes that the intensity of dialogue is an "encounter 'on the narrow ridge' in which the slightest inattention could result in a precipitous fall. Dialogue is indeed this kind of intense, high-risk encounter" (Ikeda 2005, 4). In other words, it takes courage to engage in direct encounters with the other, to constantly aspire to develop heartfelt, humanistic communication and to allow dialogue to be open-ended, rather than be outcome driven. One-to-one dialogue is a risk of a different kind to the risks or dangers written about social networking. The risks in such face-to-face dialogue are of vulnerability or exposure. Moving beyond caricatures and pre-judgments requires a willingness to be open and perhaps an admission of imperfection or frailty. Also, it is an ever-evolving process of learning to empathize rather than critically judging the other and coming to the realization that espousing theoretical knowledge is not the prime driver of profound dialogue. In a sense, dialogue is a leap of faith. While social networking serves a purpose, it is limited in its capacity to build character in the way that direct face-to-face dialogue does, and, as Ikeda argues, one-to-one dialogue is essential for the flourishing of a new humanism.

In contrast, it can be easy to abstract dialogue partners in the virtual world. It is possible to not respond or "cut off" communication, make anonymous aggressive comments or "deface" a site that does not correspond with one's worldviews without facing the suffering at the other end of the computer. It is in this context of increasing virtual communication that young people seeking one-to-one dialogue and encounters with the other are remarkable.

It is all the more significant that young people are actively engaged in such efforts at dialogue as many scholars associate young people with unhealthy risk. Examples include living at the cutting edge of a risk society, in Ulrich Beck's terms (1992), and engaging in risky behavior with few "secure psychological, economic or intellectual markers" to guide them, as Henry Giroux has pointed out in his critical pedagogy (1994, 287). Beck's thesis on risk is often applied to the precarious circumstances of vulnerable youth. Giroux's thesis of an abandoned generation also highlighted how young people are scapegoats for a culture driven by a politics of fear, expressed in racial and class discrimination, and social and political anxieties that are projected on to them (Giroux 2003, xvi). Ikeda too writes in his 2004 Peace Proposal of a tendency of young people to engage in self-destructive behavior. This he perceives as a result of young people's loss of opportunity to gain self-mastery as less meaning is placed on the traditional frameworks of family, education and local community in providing education for living. He links the danger of the increasing disconnection and "the malaise that we see infecting the hearts of so many young people" to the "cool disengagement of modern, high-tech warfare" (Ikeda 2004, 6). That is to say, young people's disengagement from local community and their retreat to virtual communication is reflective of the increasingly virtualized world of warfare where the suffering of individuals is totally obscured. Young people also tell us much about the health of society at large, as Ikeda writes:

> I think the self-destructive behavior of young people can best be understood as a dire warning about the general health of society. Their greater sensitivity renders them more vulnerable to the toxins of modern life, similar to the canaries traditionally placed in coal mines whose distress would indicate the presence of poisonous gases (Ibid., 14).

From this perspective, examples of positive engagement by young people in efforts for dialogue provide a hopeful example of the seemingly slow movement toward peace through dialogue.

The group discussion meeting

SGI organizations were established when Ikeda began to focus his leadership beyond Japan; his travels documented in the novel *The New Human Revolution* began with a visit to Hawai'i in 1960. In particular, he wanted to affirm the principle of adapting to local customs and that the refutation aspect of "shakubuku" (attempts to convert through the pointing out of errors in religious debate) was inappropriate in countries that had little exposure to the different schools of Buddhist thought. As SGI president, Ikeda looked to create a movement based on dialogue, led by his own example and the success of Soka Gakkai in Japan which had experienced phenomenal growth through the establishment of local district discussion meetings. These discussion meetings sometimes have up to 60 attendees, requiring a master of ceremonies and a formatted agenda. This style of conducting discussion meetings may vary from country to country, but where the large numbers and the model set by Japan is followed, more formally structured meetings become the norm. In countries where the district discussion meetings are attended by fewer people, dialogue can be more open-ended and inclusive of all the participants.

SGI Australia has gone through a process of transforming this heritage of the district discussion meeting to one of holding smaller group dialogues of five to ten people, allowing for all participants to be included. As with other countries, this local activity is held in members' homes. These groups of five to ten people provide a community network of support and care for its membership, as well as a forum for people interested in the philosophy of Buddhism. However, there is no formal agenda to these meetings and no particular emphasis on religious formality or gaining theoretical understanding. Rather, these support networks are experiential, emphasizing the sharing of personal experience as the means by which individuals engage in their own human revolution or inner transformation, while supporting others in the same process. Listening, sharing experiences, articulating struggles, goals and aspirations make these smaller forums ideal settings for people to learn how to apply the principles of Buddhism to everyday realities. Rather than teaching the Buddhist principle of treasuring the potential and inherent dignity of each individual's life lecture-style, these forums, and the contact that is encouraged in between the meetings, are the enactments of it.

The founding principles are care, empathy and providing a supportive environment. That is how the group meeting becomes practice, as much as personal prayer or study of theory. The consistency of regularly holding group discussion meetings also makes them a unique contribution to challenging the isolation experienced by many people. In an age driven by increasingly virtualized communication and the tendency of people suffering depression, which is experienced at almost chronic levels in Australia, to be isolated, the group discussion provides a significant community network.

Furthermore, with no specific outcome to the group discussion, dialogue is the means and the end. This allows countless opportunities for people to gain new perspectives on their personal struggles as the interaction is in part a process of self-reflection. Also, empathizing with the other fosters deep listening, which enables tendencies of disconnection, separation and depression to be broken down. Through this, many participants find relief from their suffering and are encouraged to challenge their circumstances. It is also a self-directed process of inner transformation, as these youth SGI members state in their accounts of participating in the group meetings:

> **Edward:** By participating in the group meetings, I discovered a part of me that I had not realized about myself. Being amongst a group of people and sharing the trials and tribulations of our lives and Buddhist practice showed me many things about the people there, but also something about myself. I found that I was not a particularly good or empathetic listener. I am more technical or logical about my thoughts and eager to advise. But through my continued engagement in the meetings, I learned that truly listening to that person was such a remarkably powerful skill and difficult to master. I began listening to another not by the sound or sight of their expression, but through the heart and courage within myself. Through this, I was really able to engage and share with that person.

The experience of the group discussion meeting spills over into how young people approach situations of discomfort in their daily life, as Tiffany shares:

> **Tiffany:** The group has really taught me to be open and compassionate to people I would normally avoid because we didn't get along. There was a particular person at work, whom I always clashed with and always hated dealing with. I would not want to work with her and always felt dread at having any work projects together. Our meetings discussed how we should always make an effort, not just with people that it's easy for us to get along with, but with people who challenge us and I decided to make a conscious effort with one person at work whom I had struggled with. I feel we now have a

much better working relationship and I no longer feel the dread
when we have to work together.

This form of training or character development, by taking an active role in
supporting each other in the process of inner transformation, is a key element
of what the group discussion meeting offers to participants. These young
people highlight that it is an extremely valuable forum where dialogue drives
empathy for the other. It also challenges self-doubt and the devaluing of one's
significance that often underpins self-destructive behavior.

> **Lisa:** When we reach out to another member, we are showing our
> care, belief and trust in them. It is from this determined, appreciative
> behaviour that we gain the strength and courage to keep going in
> the face of all our negativity, fears and what our environment seem-
> ingly throws at us. When our self-doubt threatens to drag us down,
> we can share this with a fellow member and trust in their support
> and care. This heart-to-heart dialogue, sincere encouragement and
> belief in the person in front of us reminds us of our own unlimited
> potential for joy and happiness.

As mentioned, the group discussion could be seen as a model of the "ideal
speech community" in Habermas's theory of communicative rationality;
however, it is much more than that. It is providing a solid community
network with no self-interest involved. The nature of dialogue counters the
encroachment of dogmatism and fanaticism, ensuring its egalitarian foundation. The ongoing evolution of SGI Australia's group discussion meetings
can also be considered "postreligious" in that the emphasis has shifted away
from theoretical knowledge being imparted lecture-style to one of humanistic expression modeled on the founder's behavior of dialogue as the prime
expression of humanism. Of perhaps greater significance, these egalitarian
forums are an expression of Ikeda's legacy, which SGI will take a future role
in conveying to future generations. They are a contemporary expression of the
essence of Buddhism as a life-affirming philosophy that has proven attrac-
tive for young people to engage in, and participation by young people has
increased dramatically since their inception.

SGI Youth and Muslim Youth exchanges

In December 2005, a highly charged event occurred on a well-known surfing beach in Sydney. It has come to be referred to as the Cronulla riots, and it tested Australia's pride in its multicultural record. Purportedly the event was sparked by a couple of young Middle Eastern men who assaulted some Caucasian surf lifesavers. The symbolism of this would not be lost outside Australia. Tensions lasted over a week and much media attention was given to the way in which hundreds of angry young men organized using social media networking to retaliate. The media were seen as proactive in drawing conclusions as to the racially driven nature of the week-long violence that ensued (Lehmann 2005). With the distance of time some social critics came to view the race issue as overblown, suggesting that it may have been a small, isolated incident; part of a "turf war" in a surfing culture dominated by young males (Nettle 2010). However, the events highlighted the need to move beyond caricatures of differences and create opportunities for meaningful dialogues. Widespread misconceptions faced by Muslim youth, as well as the struggle for inclusion in what is referred to as "mainstream" Australia, form the context within which the following program can be viewed as making a contribution centered on dialogue.

"Why dialogue?" is the title of one chapter of *Global Civilization: A Buddhist–Islamic Dialogue*. This dialogue between Ikeda and Tehranian forms part of an unprecedented body of work for peace that has been driven by Ikeda's conviction that dialogue is the "weapon of peace" (Ikeda and Tehranian 2003, 9). Their beliefs originate at geographically opposite spectrums of the culturally rich Silk Road. In their dialogue, they share the tension within their own spiritual traditions between the tendencies of cementing legality, an emphasis on theoretical understanding and formalism and that of spirituality or the essence of their teachings as guides for living well. Both employ the metaphor of dialogue as light, and of self-righteousness, untested by the rigor of dialogue, as darkness. They both share confidence in the common ground of humanity as the basis for overcoming a "friend vs. foe" mentality in interactions with different civilizations and for preventing fanatics from misinterpreting the founding spirit of their respective religious beliefs. This dialogue, conducted from 1992 to 2000, prior to the events of

September 11 – a defining event that appeared to cement a "friend vs. foe" mentality between the West and Islam – offers a profound model of dialogue that transcends differences and challenges the notion of the inevitability of a "clash of civilizations."

Inner dialogue as a prerequisite

As mentioned, in his 2002 Peace Proposal Ikeda, despite a climate when the motivation for promoting dialogue was being questioned, calls for an inner dialogue to guide responses to the events of 9/11.

> In the darkness in which our civilization has been immersed since September 11, we sense an eerie absence, a spiritual landscape in which people are failing to recognize the humanity of the other. It is far from easy to engage in meaningful dialogue in this climate, for it is the consciousness of an internalized other within the self that gives life to dialogue. An inner, spiritual dialogue is a necessary prerequisite for any attempt at external dialogue. Unless such attempts are preceded and supported by inner dialogue, we may find ourselves reverting to mere monologue and one-sided assertions. In its most advanced state, the pathology of the absent other converts language and speech into just another form of violence (Ikeda 2002, 15).

This call to internalize the other, rather than make them absent, applies to reflecting on the increasing world of virtual communication as well as the dehumanizing processes at play when abstracting the other. The process of inner dialogue is guided by self-reflection and acknowledging the need for dialogue to be a process of learning about the other. It is the challenge of not reverting to monologues explaining or justifying one's own position. Holding on to a position forms the grounds for debate or, at its worst, violence and we are exposed to these forms of monologue in political discourse. Ikeda encourages a different approach; one that is possible with inner dialogue as a prerequisite. Referring back to Giroux, young Muslims have been treated as scapegoats and often misrepresented in mainstream media in societies increasingly driven by fear. The following example of ongoing exchanges between an SGI youth group and young Muslims participating in a leadership training program highlights the potential of dialogue for internalizing the other and sharing the "common ground of humanity" (Tehranian and Ikeda 2003, 9).

Annually, over the past three years (2008–10), a dialogue has been held between a group of SGI Australia Youth Leaders and Muslim Youth Leaders. The event is a component of a 10-day leadership program of LaTrobe University specifically designed for Muslim youth. The program's aims is to encourage the participants to reach their full potential as citizens and future leaders through a study tour that exposes them to government institutions, media outlets as well as religious and community organizations. As part of the program, the group of Muslim Youth visits the SGI Australia Culture Centre for an exchange with a youth leadership group of SGI Australia. Initially this was an evening event of a few hours over dinner, with brief introductions and explanations around their faith traditions. The second year was a half-day event with more exchange about how their faith drives their social interaction in the community. The third year was a full day event, which included a panel discussion, the viewing of an exhibition about depression and exchanges from both groups of their experiences of depression, violence and social pressures. This shift to finding commonalities based on shared struggles they face as young people fueled a greater connection on the "common ground of humanity" (Ikeda, op. cit). Feedback from the event was sought with the interviewees being asked questions around the following themes: (1) whether their misperceptions of the other group were challenged; (2) their views on the contribution of dialogue to peace; (3) what they learnt from the other; and, (4) how viewing a special exhibition on depression contributed to the depth of dialogue.

(1) The question about misperceptions was framed as follows.

Were they any misperceptions you held about the other group of participants that were dispelled on the day? What was the nature of these misperceptions?

The responses demonstrated sensitivity, as well as a willingness to learn about the other group and go beyond the initial perceptions that they may have had. Other respondents, not quoted here, shared a common desire to engage with the other group and from both groups there were comments as to how each faith informed a way of living that was not theoretically driven.

> **TK (SGI):** The main misperception I had before meeting the other participants came from an expectation that there would be a slight chip on their shoulder, you know, a heavy sense of disappointment with the constant misrepresentation that occurs in the media and public sphere about their faith and the people practicing their faith. Instead, what I encountered with them was a spirit of generosity and warmth that inspired me to have more confidence in my own faith and practice as well as my own mission to contribute to my community.

> **Nobuko (SGI):** About Islam and women. I didn't know women's rights are clearly stated in the Koran.

And, with more humor:

> **Nadeem (MY):** I think many people associate Buddhists with bald Asian people! So certainly this was dispelled!

(2) Their views on dialogue were sought with the following question:

What did you learn from your interactions on the day about dialogue and its contribution to peace?

On the whole their responses aligned with Ikeda's views on dialogue and the importance placed on the human encounter, understanding each other and empathy toward the other, or as Nadeem, from the Muslim Youth Leadership Program succinctly put it: "Certainly dialogue plays an integral part – I feel its most important contribution is in humanizing 'the other.'" The two responses quoted below also illustrate that the objective of the day, to engage in a humanistic dialogue planned around Ikeda's ideas of dialogue, was being achieved and acknowledged as effective.

> **Ayam (MY):** I think dialogue is really the only way forward towards peace and to have effective dialogue we need to really understand the

other. Even if our points of view differ we need to really put ourselves in the other person's shoes and empathize and try and understand where they are coming from. Only then will we achieve true dialogue and the peace movement can go forward. Dialogue is not about one's monologue but it is really about being gracefully attentive to each other. Working in cooperation to build a better world.

TK (SGI): Anytime in the future that I am led to believe there is another, "easier" approach to a truly meaningful coexistence with other people in my life and community that promises to be more effective than dialogue, I have this particular day to prove otherwise. Even as I am recalling the events of the day right now, I feel emboldened and re-determined to live in a way that demands the deep engagement with the person in front of me that I did not know but did achieve on that day.

(3) The following question was asked about learning from the other:

What did you learn from the other group of participants about their beliefs and how they live based on their beliefs?

Zara (MY): For me the most important lesson I learnt was that there's no shame in discussing anything about your personal life and sharing can be a really empowering gift.

Janssen (SGI): I learnt that the Muslim youth were normal human beings who were struggling like anyone else. Most of them were judged unfairly in the society by their appearance. It's through their beliefs that they were able to show compassion and transform their prejudged situations.

Nadeem (MY): To be honest, I spent most of the day talking about normal everyday non-religious stuff!!

Other comments referred to the openness with which each group shared their struggles to express their faith in society. The Muslim Youth were struck by the way SGI members spoke about their journeys of coming to the practice and so openly shared very personal experiences. One of the aims of the event was to shift dialogue from comparing each other's faith to learning about the humanity of the other. Another aim was to find commonalities in experiences such as the challenges involved in sharing their faith with their friends, or enduring various types of social pressure, as well as violence and depression. "Dark to Dawn: Being Creative about Depression" is an exhibition with themes of offering hopeful perspectives and challenging perceptions about the nature of depression. This was exhibited as a way of focusing the dialogue away from comparing faiths and to open up the creative possibilities of dialogue.

(4) The following question was asked about its contribution to the day.

What did the Exhibit (Dark to Dawn: Being Creative about Depression) contribute to the day's events?

> **Ayam (MY):** I thought it was really interesting (coming from a depression background myself). I liked the idea of creating a space for dialogue in which you could express yourself creatively. The idea is similar to Art Therapy and the notion that creative thought can be used as a therapeutic tool is one that deserves a lot more time and merit.

> **TK (SGI):** It helped to focus the whole day's discussion on the human condition. In our little group dialogues we were able to share openly our inner struggles to confront our negativity, from the point of view of faith but more memorably through unique individual experiences in growing as young people. Amazing.

> **Zara (MY):** I think it set the scene for the last part of the day and the panel that we had. I had a really hard time holding my end due to some personal issues. But I felt the support of all the members of the panel and afterwards during discussions.

Janssen (SGI): The awareness in giving hope to those who are suffering from depression and it gave great discussion points when we broke up into small group discussions.

Showing the depression exhibition helped in shifting the dialogue to one of sharing struggles and personal experiences, and focusing on the human condition. The final comment in regard to this exchange is by one of the Muslim Youth participants who told the audience he had been invited to many multi-faith forums, but said this one was "unique and revolutionary."

In summary, these two examples of an innovative multi-faith dialogue and the group discussion provide the hopeful possibility that Ikeda has persistently promoted, namely that dialogue is indeed the weapon of peace and that "In any society, in any country, in any civilization, the vast majority of people reject extremist views" (Ikeda 2005, 24). In conclusion, Greg Johns, SGI Australia General Director wrote of his belief in Ikeda's legacy and how it is epitomized in the dialogue movement in SGI Australia:

> Dialogue opens a window to engaging with life itself. (...) The best opportunity for heart-to-heart dialogue exists where there is a sense of community, where one is not judged and can freely engage in expressing one's thoughts and emotions. Within the SGI movement, the local discussion meeting is the practical realization of this ideal. In this space people from any background or experience can gather and share their victories and woes in an environment of inclusiveness and creative dialogue. Such encounters develop from a vision of community as the creative "space" where dialogue is treasured and the action of self-transformation forms the foundation of hope for humanity as a whole (Johns 2007, 5).

Ikeda has shown through his example and life's work that building community is a painstaking, yet extraordinarily valuable, process. The methodology of small group dialogues is creating a groundswell of humanistic expression centered on encouragement to engage with people from all kinds of background. This chapter has aimed to introduce the exciting possibilities of engaging young people in embarking on the rigorous and risky challenge of dialogue. That young people can learn about the self-transformative process of face-to-face dialogue makes it a significant training ground and offers a hopeful orientation toward breaking down barriers of differences. With the focus of discussion being a search for the "common ground of humanity," as opposed perhaps to limiting discussions to comparisons of faith traditions, there are myriad possibilities for community building. It is recognizing and enacting dialogue as a practice, in the way Ikeda continues to demonstrate, that ensures dialogue does not only occur in ideal settings. Fortunately, Ikeda does not set down specifics of "how to" or list strategies for the practice of dialogue. Rather, he presents a rich and profound pool of wisdom from which we can learn how individual and collective creativity may blossom in risky encounter.

PART III

DIALOGIC PRACTICE IN EDUCATION

CHAPTER 5

Daisaku Ikeda and Dialogue *on* Education, *in* Education and *as* Education

Jason Goulah

> Peace starts with dialogue.
> – Daisaku Ikeda (2010b)

> The path of education is one of continuous trailblazing.
> As long as there is misery in the world, we must never cease
> our efforts in that regard. Indeed, the true purpose and
> mission of education is to overcome human suffering.
> – Daisaku Ikeda (2008, 243)

Introduction

An edited volume on Daisaku Ikeda's philosophy and practice of dialogue, what I have elsewhere called "value-creative dialogue" (Goulah 2012), is long overdue. As a Japanese peace activist, school founder and Buddhist leader, Ikeda has engaged in more than 7,000 dialogues with world leaders and thinkers in numerous fields and religious faiths; more than 50 of these have been published as full-length books. Dialogue serves as the cornerstone of Ikeda's annual (since 1983) peace proposals and is a guiding framework of the secular Soka schools he founded (Soka schools include kindergartens in Brazil, Japan, Hong Kong, Korea, Malaysia and Singapore; elementary schools in Brazil and Japan; secondary schools in Japan; and colleges and universities in Japan and the United States). Universities around the world have consistently cited Ikeda's promotion of and reliance on dialogue for peaceful and creative coexistence in awarding him more than 300 honorary doctorates and professorships.

Elsewhere, I (Goulah 2012) have examined the role of dialogue in Nichiren Buddhism, the school of Buddhism Ikeda practices, and Tsunesaburo Makiguchi's (1871–1944) theory of value creation (*soka*) as theoretical frameworks for understanding Ikeda's dialogic approach. I have also considered the multiple roles that Ikeda's dialogues play: as an individual interculturalism between Ikeda and his interlocutor(s); as a broader conduit for intercultural dialogue between the 12 million members of Soka Gakkai International (SGI), the Buddhist nongovernmental organization Ikeda leads, and his interlocutor(s), and between those interlocutors and Ikeda's mentor, Josei Toda, and his mentor's mentor, Tsunesaburo Makiguchi, respectively the second and first presidents of the Soka Gakkai; and as a model for SGI members' own individual dialogues at their local level(s). I do not reiterate those arguments here. Instead, as Ikeda has vowed to make education the "ultimate of [his] undertakings" (1978, 162; cf. Ikeda 1980, 104), I examine Ikeda's approach to dialogue *on* education, *in* education, and *as* education for peace and social policy.

Specifically, I consider Ikeda's philosophy of dialogue and education through a Bakhtinian lens, which is gradually emerging as a foundational theory in education. Thereafter, I excerpt Ikeda's dialogues with world educators and with students to identify emergent themes intersecting dialogue, peace and education in the Ikeda corpus. Because of limited space, I restrict my discussions in the former category to Ikeda's dialogues with Russian educator and rector of Moscow State University, Victor Sadovnichy (Sadovnichy and Ikeda 2004), professor of Chinese history and Confucianism at Harvard University, Tu Weiming (Ikeda and Tu 2007), Danish educator and former principal of the Askov Folk High School, Hans Henningsen (Henningsen and Ikeda 2009), American educators and John Dewey scholars, Larry Hickman and Jim Garrison (Hickman, Garrison and Ikeda 2009–10), and Taiwanese educator and chair of Taiwan's Chinese Culture University Board of Regents, Chang Jen-Hu (Ikeda and Chang 2010). In the latter case, I focus on Ikeda's dialogues with students enrolled at the Soka schools he founded (e.g. Ikeda 2010a).

Theoretical framework

This article is couched theoretically in the concept of heteroglossia advanced by Russian literary critic and philologist, Mikhail Bakhtin (1895–1975). Bakhtin scholar Michael Holquist (2004) calls heteroglossia "dialogism," and although Ikeda has never characterized his approach to dialogue in Bakhtinian terms, I believe Bakhtin's dialogism provides one of the best lenses for conceptualizing Ikeda's view, purpose and practice of dialogue for peace – especially in the context of education. There are two interrelated reasons for this belief: First, for Bakhtin – and for Ikeda – human beings are fundamentally interdependent with one another and all other phenomena. In other words, Holquist (1986, xix) contends that for Bakhtin, "Our very status as the subjects of our own lives depends on the necessary presence of other subjects." Elsewhere, Holquist asserts, "Whatever else it is, self/other [in Bakhtin's philosophy] is a relation of simultaneity" (Holquist 2004, 19). Likewise, Ikeda, grounded in the Buddhist concepts of *esho funi* and *engi*, or the inseparability and dependent origination of self and other, states: "A truer, fuller sense of self is found in the totality of the psyche that is inextricably linked to 'other'" (Ikeda 2001, 41). Ikeda goes on to say that "Human beings only fully exist in their relations with others" (Ikeda 2003/2006, 127).

Second, Bakhtin argues the optimal – indeed, only – way to fully develop the self, then, is through dialogic interaction with the other; and the other can only be fully developed dialogically with the self. In other words, Holquist contends, "in [Bakhtin's] dialogism, the very capacity to have consciousness is based on otherness (…) in dialogism consciousness is otherness" (Holquist 2004, 18). In this sense, dialogism is "not mere verbal exchange between interlocutors; it is a complex world that stresses the interconnectedness and permeability of symbolic and physical boundaries" (Vitanova 2005, 158) as a means of personal development – *dialogic becoming*. Ikeda echoes this Bakhtinian view in his own characterization of dialogue between the self and other:

> It is only in the burning furnace of intense, soul-baring exchanges
> – the ceaseless and mutually supporting processes of inner and outer
> dialogue between one's 'self' and a profoundly internalized 'other' –
> that our beings are tempered and refined. Only then can we begin

to grasp and fully affirm the reality of being alive. Only then can we bring forth the brilliance of a universal spirituality that embraces all humankind (Ikeda 2001, 43).

Ikeda juxtaposes such dialogic becoming with a "false," monologic sense of dialogue:

> Exchanges between two individuals both lacking a sense of "other" might appear to be dialogue but are in fact simply the trading of one-sided statements. Communication inevitably fails. Most distressing in this kind of semantic space – at once voluble and empty – is that words lose their resonance and are eventually stifled and expire. The demise of words naturally means the demise of an essential aspect of our humanity – the capacity for language that earned us the name *Homo loquens* (speaking man) (Ibid., 42).

In terms of education in its truest sense, then, dialogic becoming is paramount for fostering peace. Bakhtin expands upon this sense of dialogic becoming in his discussions of the *Bildungsroman*,[1] what he called "the novel of educa-tion" (Bakhtin 1986, 19). For Bakhtin, the *Bildungsroman* was one of the best and most educative types of novel because it reveals "man in the process of becoming" (Ibid., 21) and "emerg[ing] along with the [social] world and (...) reflecting] the historical emergence of the world itself" (Ibid., 23). Bakhtin argues that "the very idea of man's becoming and developing (...) makes necessary a generous and full representation of the social worlds, voices, languages of the era, among which the hero's becoming – the result of his testing and his choices – is accomplished" (Bakhtin 1981, 411). Examples of *Bildungsromans* that come to mind here are Johann Wolfgang von Goethe's *The Apprenticeship of Wilhelm Meister* (1795–96), Charlotte Bronte's *Jane Eyre* (1847), Jean-Jacques Rousseau's *Emile* (1762) and James Joyce's *A Portrait of the Artist as a Young Man* (1916).

For Ikeda, such dialogic becoming in the evolving social world – what for him may be called a form of human education (*ningen kyoiku*) – is the ultimate form of peace. That is, while Ikeda of course envisions peace in the termination of nuclear weapons, violence, limited human rights, environmental degradation, and so forth, I believe he sees these obstacles to peace as larger manifestations of people's fundamental inability to *dialogically become* in the Bakhtinian sense (Ikeda 1993/1996). Ikeda views such dialogic becoming as an internal human revolution from the monologic "lesser self" to the dialogic "greater self" forged through interpersonal, intercultural, and interlingual interaction:

> If people were to pursue dialogue in an equally unrelenting manner, the inevitable conflicts of human life would surely find easier resolution. Prejudice would yield to empathy and war would give way to peace. Genuine dialogue results in the transformation of opposing viewpoints, changing them from wedges that drive people apart into bridges that link them together (Ibid., 156).

Ikeda's goal in and outside education is to help individuals recognize and realize their greater selves through dialogue, for only when all individuals in the world become so empowered will peaceful coexistence occur. As Ikeda states in one of his books on education:

> Our daily lives are filled with opportunities to develop ourselves and those around us. Each of our interactions with others – dialogue, exchange and participation – is an invaluable chance to create value. We learn from people and it is for this reason that the humanity of the teacher represents the core of educational experience (Ikeda 2001, 105).

Moreover, I think it is in Ikeda's own concrete examples of dialogue *on*, *in* and *as* education that Bakhtin's theory of dialogic becoming is both realized and best exemplified at micro and macro levels.

In the next section I draw from Ikeda's dialogues on education to illustrate his views about the importance of dialogue in education and as education for peace and social policy.

Daisaku Ikeda and dialogue *on*, *in* and *as* education
Dialogue with world educators

A number of Ikeda's published dialogues were conducted with educators and focus specifically on education; however, only one of these has been translated into English (Derbolav and Ikeda 1992). Therefore, in this section I excerpt[2] passages from Ikeda's dialogues on education unavailable in English in which he and his interlocutor(s) articulate the role of dialogue *in* and *as* education for peace at a macro level (I consider Ikeda's views at a micro level in the following section). By macro level, I mean Ikeda's views about dialogue and education for peace at conceptual or philosophical levels. Here, it is important to remember that as the founder of the Soka schools network, Ikeda is certainly an informed intellectual concerned with the goals and institutionalization of education in broad terms; however, he explicitly does not weigh in on issues of curriculum, methodology and so forth, stating: "As one person earnestly desiring the wholesome growth and development of youth, I cannot help being anxious. Since I am not a specialist [read: teacher-practitioner] in the field, I have no intention of discussing individual educational methods or the various aspects of the educational system that require reform" (Ikeda 2001, 123–24). Thus, this section focuses on Ikeda's view of dialogue and peace education in a broad sense; that is, its role in the full development of humankind. Here the value of Soka education and Ikeda's aim in establishing the Soka schools is relevant: "The ultimate goal of Soka, or value-creating, education is to foster people of character who continuously strive for the greatest good – that of peace – who are committed to protecting the sanctity of life and who are capable of creating value under even the most difficult circumstances" (Ibid., 115).

Finally, scrutiny of Ikeda's dialogues quickly reveals that as he engages his immediate interlocutor(s), here on issues of dialogue, peace and education, he can be seen simultaneously facilitating an implicit, larger dialogue across or among his interlocutors on those very subjects. In this sense, Ikeda brings together all his interlocutors, over time and space, on issues necessary to cultivate the full flower of humanity. At the same time, by doing so, he illustrates for readers that a commitment to dialogue, education and peace is shared by great thinkers of various faiths, languages and cultures in the East, West, and in-between. Below, I use this concept of inter-dialogue dialogism to present Ikeda's views on the key elements of dialogue and education for peace emerging from his interactions with the aforementioned educators.

Ikeda and Henningsen

In his dialogue with Danish educator Hans Henningsen (Henningsen and Ikeda 2009, 121) Ikeda asserts, "Education is a task that requires great patience. It aims to provide the energy to convert the delusions of malice, despair, ignorance and resignation into the wisdom of compassion, hope, intelligence and courage." This concept is most explicitly explored relative to dialogue in the final chapter entitled "Peace Education and the Great Light of Dialogue." In this chapter Ikeda states, "For me, peace is essential. And it is education that is the foundation of constructing peace" (Ibid., 313). He and Henningsen conclude that their shared focus on peace education lies in their having experienced the tragedy of World War II. Ikeda's four older brothers were sent to the front; the eldest was killed in action in Burma. Ikeda states: "Earlier we discussed our experiences in times of war. I believe that as people who have lived through the twentieth century, the century of war, it is our mission and responsibility to convey to future generations the preciousness of peace and the brutality of war. Isn't that also the purpose of the important work of peace education?" (Ibid., 313–14). Thereafter, Ikeda praises Henningsen for taking up the renowned Danish thinker N.F.S. Grundtvig's (1783–1872) spiritual struggle for "education for peace" and "dialogue for peace." He then inquires, "Isn't what's lacking today [in education] the type of dialogue that is based on language of the heart?" (Ibid., 331). Henningsen concurs: "The school is a place where people are able to discover through dialogue the fundamental aspect they share as human beings – the dignity of human life" (Ibid.). Ikeda replies: "Indeed. Education and dialogue must become keywords" (Ibid.), and "Opposition and conflict only result in a vicious cycle. Without advancing dialogue we cannot change the situation. Based on 'dialogue,' we must bring about change and open a new path toward the idea of soft power. The role of education in creating peace based on dialogue is unfathomable" (Ibid., 331). In these exchanges on education, Ikeda's value of dialogue in and as education for peace is evident.

From Ikeda and Henningsen to Ikeda and Hickman and Garrison

In addition to Ikeda and Henningsen's discussions of dialogue in education and as education for peace, Ikeda recounts for Henningsen the backdrop of militaristic education in Japan that glorified the war. Arguing that we must learn from history and not repeat its mistakes, he then asks Henningsen what type of peace education is offered in Danish schools. Henningsen replies simply that peace education in Denmark aims at preparing students for a democratic life, asserting that the democratic political system is essential for realizing peace.

This intersection of democracy with dialogue and education for peace represents a lynchpin of sorts in Ikeda's dialogism across dialogues, for he revisits this intersection in a later dialogue with American educators and John Dewey scholars, Larry Hickman and Jim Garrison (e.g. Hickman et al. 2009). This latter dialogue focuses on commonalities between Soka education and Deweyan philosophy. In the opening section titled "It is in Dialogue that Real Value is Created," Ikeda begins with the following:

> "Democracy begins with dialogue." So declared John Dewey in a speech at his 90th birthday party. These words crystallize the ideology of America's foremost philosopher and educator, John Dewey. Without "dialogue" to open the heart, the human spirit would wither and cease to grow. Without the free "flow of spirit," society would become rigid and stuck. Dewey clearly articulated the path of improving and developing human beings and society (Ibid., 53).

This idea at once picks up Henningsen's aforementioned theme of democracy and peace education and resonates with Ikeda's own earlier thinking:

> But spiritual freedom does not mean spiritual license. It does not mean thinking and acting in a willful, arbitrary manner. True devel-opment can take place only in the presence of both expansive liberty and a high degree of self-discipline. In my view this means the opportunity to grow by sharing ideas through dialogue, provoking and catalyzing each other toward an expanded field of vision and ultimately to profound and encompassing insight into the nature of things (Ikeda 1973/2006, 28).

Moreover, the above passages indicate not only Ikeda's personal views but also his agreement with Henningsen that peace education requires a type of dialogue that seeks democratic and social becoming. And by introducing this topic through a Deweyan lens in his dialogue with Hickman and Garrison, he brings it – and, in this sense, his dialogue with Henningsen – to them in the context of their scholarly discipline. This is an important and consistent dialogic aspect that Ikeda employs across his dialogues.

In a subsequent installment of the Ikeda, Hickman and Garrison dialogue (Hickman et al. 2010), this dialogic thread comes full circle to its starting point of militaristic education. Garrison notes, in light of their discussions on war, that it is interesting that although we have military academies we do not have "peace schools" where students deeply consider and comprehend peace. Ikeda agrees and contends that creating such peace schools is indeed the task of the twenty-first century.

From Ikeda and Hickman and Garrison to Ikeda and Tu and Chang

After discussing peace schools, Ikeda, Hickman and Garrison turn to the topic of cultivating peace through international exchange and intercultural interaction. This line is anticipated in Ikeda's dialogue with Chinese scholar Tu Weiming in their aptly titled dialogue, *Civilization of Dialogue: On the Hope-filled Philosophy of Peace* (Ikeda and Tu 2007). Here, the topic of dialogue is central, and in terms of peace, the interlocutors focus on the need for East–West dialogue and cultural exchange on national and individual levels. Ikeda asserts that in addition to understanding differences in the other's values and cultural and political traditions, tenacious pursuit of dialogue and exchange is indispensable for fostering peace and creative coexistence. In making this argument, Ikeda references two passages from Tu in the opening pages of their dialogue. These passages become important themes throughout their dialogue and can be traced to Ikeda's subsequent dialogues. The first reference reads, "Dialogue is an important mechanism for erasing contradictions and collisions between civilizations" (Ikeda and Tu 2007, 11). The second states: "The mechanism of dialogue that recognizes the other's existence, respects the value and right of that existence, learns in comparison with one another, and receives benefit from each other, is essential between differing civilizations"

(Ibid., 11–12). Ikeda and Tu conclude by envisioning a "civilization of dialogue" whereby a new intercultural dialogism based on a universal framework of communities bound in dialogue, or "communities of dialogue" (*taiwa no kyodotai*), is necessary.

As with Hickman and Garrison, Ikeda agrees with Tu that youth exchange is the best means for creating peaceful friendship across cultures and for moving from a "civilization of teaching" (*oshieru bunmei*) to a "civilization of learning" (*manabu bunmei*) (Ibid., 283).

As mentioned above, Ikeda revisits this evolving thread of civilizations of dialogue with Taiwanese scholar Chang Jen-Hu (Chang and Ikeda 2010) when they discuss the need to move from a society that recognizes "differences among civilizations" (*bunmei no sai*) to one that recognizes the "interdependence of civilizations" (*bunmei no kyosei*). Drawing on this dialogue with Tu, Ikeda references Tu's focus on Confucian benevolence and offers the following to Chang: "How can we move from a 'civilization of difference' to a 'civilization of interdependence,' a 'civilization of dialogue'? How can we discover that 'life' has the greatest value and create a universal 'culture of peace' for humanity? Indeed, people of the world must together forge such a 'new spiritual Silk Road'" (Chang and Ikeda 2010, 262).

As was evident in Ikeda's articulation of terms from the Henningsen dialogue to the Hickman and Garrison dialogue, his similar adoption of terms across dialogues with Hickman, Garrison, Tu, and Chang also has importance in Bakhtinian terms. Bakhtin (1981) argues that the generation of meaning happens through heteroglossia and polyglossia and the relation between utterances. In other words, for Bakhtin, making an utterance means that we have appropriated the words of others and populated them with our own intention. I believe Ikeda's dialogism across dialogues is a prime example of this and it exemplifies a literal and, I believe, volitional Bakhtinian "dialogic becoming" for Ikeda, which he then seeks to engender, if unconsciously, for his interlocutors.

From Ikeda and Tu to Ikeda and Sadovnichy

Above, Ikeda, Tu, and Chang can be seen together envisioning a "civilization of learning." Perhaps of all the themes raised herein, this is the most conceptual or philosophical, particularly in terms of peace education. However, this notion can be seen taking shape in terms of educational policy in Ikeda's idea of "society for education" rather than "education for society." The idea of society for education occupies a large portion of Ikeda's dialogue with Moscow State University rector Victor Sadovnichy (Sadovnichy and Ikeda 2004) and is not new to scholars of Ikeda's educational philosophy. Ikeda has elsewhere addressed various aspects of this idea in Japanese (e.g. Ikeda 2003; 2004) and English (Ikeda 2001).

The main thrust of Ikeda's proposal to shift the vector of influence stems from his having experienced militaristic education bent on preparing children to be subjects of the state. Instead, he entreats society to focus on education to cultivate the essential needs of human beings; that is, to foster their full dialogic becoming. Engaging Sadovnichy, Ikeda suggests that "Rather than having 'the state' and then 'education,' there is first 'education,' then 'the state.' Education creates the structure of 'humanity'; then from that humanity there is society, industry and government. Viewing things in a way where 'first there is politics and economics, then somewhere supporting that is education' is putting the cart before the horse" (Ikeda 2001, 18–19). I believe Ikeda sees such a fundamental shift in the purposes of education to be the main route for fostering a civilization of learning and a civilization of dialogue. Moreover, I think here we cannot forget Ikeda's role as founder of the Soka schools and Sadovnichy's as rector of a major world university. Assuredly cognizant of these realities, Ikeda engages Sadovnichy in deep reflection about the fundamental purpose of educating human beings in general and in the twenty-first century in particular.

In a joint introduction, Sadovnichy and Ikeda agree: "We can say that today's educational world has accomplished, in general, a common vision of how curriculum and the school system should be; however, there is a disparity in perception as to what the purpose of education and the nature of subjects' content ought to be" (Sadovnichy and Ikeda 2004, 5). It is clear, however, in examining the totality of Ikeda's writings and dialogues on education that he views the ultimate mission of society and education to be the cultivation of peace, happiness and the full development of humankind.

In the next section I examine Ikeda's dialogues with students enrolled at the Soka schools he founded. In particular I consider their treatment of bullying, which continues to be a major problem in Japan and the USA (e.g. Freibert 2010; Ikeda 2001).

Ikeda and dialogue with students: On bullying

In this section, I move from Ikeda's dialogues with world educators to his dialogues with students enrolled in the Soka schools he founded. In so doing, I concentrate on Ikeda's repeated focus on bullying, which has been a common theme in his discussions on education and represents, perhaps compared with the topics addressed above, an important micro-level issue in schooling. In other words, the topic of bullying ties together this article's themes of dialogue, education and peace in the context of students' daily lives in school. In his book *Soka Education*, Ikeda (2001, 36) argues that the focus of education – and Soka education, in particular – is and should be students' happiness. He argues:

> Scrutiny of the numbers aside, the point here is that aberrant conditions have become the norm. Children are the microcosm of the times, and, as such, they mirror the future of society. As long as these mirrors remain dark and clouded, we will not see in them a hope-filled future.
>
> While some remedial measures have been instituted by the Ministry of Education and independent commissions, I feel that along with structural deterrents to bullying there is an urgent need to establish not only in schools but throughout society an ethos of zero tolerance toward violence.

Returning for a moment to Ikeda's dialogue with Hickman and Garrison, Ikeda introduces the topic of bullying, arguing that it keeps children from feeling safe in schools and must never be ignored or silently tolerated. Garrison, who teaches at Virginia Tech, where a student tragically shot and killed peers, faculty and himself, argues that bullying can be physical, emotional, or intellectual and is a form of "social violence" (Hickman et al. 2010, 6, 63). Ikeda asserts: "The thinking that argues 'there is some kind of problem with those who are bullied' is completely wrong. Bullying is evil; those who bully are in the wrong one hundred percent. More than anything, I believe it is crucial for teachers and adults to firmly and resolutely convey to children that bullying is completely inexcusable" (Ibid., 6, 64; see also Ibid., 8).

Ikeda's views expressed in the dialogue with Hickman and Garrison are consistent with those in his earlier writings, in which he argues:

> We must end the tragedy of school violence whereby the rich seeds of future promise and potential are destroyed by the children themselves. Every time I visit the Soka schools in Tokyo and Kansai, I speak frankly with the students, stating that bullying and violence are in all cases wrong and encouraging the students that we should all work together to eliminate these evils from society (Ikeda 2001, 37).

Indeed, some of these discussions with Soka students are captured in *Discussions on Youth* (Ikeda 1998, Vols 1 & 2), which was reissued in 2010 with more recent dialogues also appended (Ikeda 2010a). In these discussions, one easily discerns Ikeda's opinion of bullying as an obstruction to peace. In *Discussions on Youth*, bullying is raised in the context of human rights. First, Ikeda asserts: "All people have a right to flower, to reveal their full potential as human beings, to fulfill their mission in this world. You have this right, and so does everyone else. This is the meaning of human rights" (Ikeda 2010a, 121). Then a youth asks Ikeda, "Discrimination and bullying exist in our immediate surroundings. At the extreme end of the scale we have war and oppression. Do you think it's safe to say that these share a common root?" Ikeda responds simply, "Yes. Some have said that bullying is just war in miniature" (Ibid., 122).

Ikeda and his youthful interlocutor continue their discussion on bullying, with the latter, like Garrison, framing it in the context of a national social malfeasance: "I understand that in most European countries, discrimination is a crime. Japan is still an underdeveloped country as far as human rights are concerned" (Ibid.). Ikeda replies: "Many, many people have said as much. Our distorted society is responsible in no small part for the bullying that plagues our schools" (Ibid.). Thereafter, the youthful interlocutor reads a series of moving testimonials from students who have been bullied, and Ikeda responds in the following way, anticipating his comments to Hickman and Garrison:

> Whatever the reason, bullying is wrong. Maybe those who bully others have their excuses – maybe they want to take out their pain on others. But whatever the reason or motive, bullying and discrimination are impossible to justify. We all need to come to an agreement that bullying is a crime against humanity. Part of the fight for human rights is standing up to those doing bad things. Another part of that fight is protecting good people (Ibid., 123).

This dialogue moves into the real and practical with the next question posed to Ikeda: "I've heard students say that when they try to put a stop to bullying, they end up being bullied themselves. Fear immobilizes them, and then they get really depressed and down on themselves because they cannot change things" (Ibid.). Ikeda encourages young people in a passage worth quoting at length:

> When you cannot get bullies to stop picking on others through your own efforts, talk to your principal, your homeroom teacher, older students whom you trust or your parents. Think of some way to improve the situation.
>
> (...) But whatever happens, you must not get down on yourself if you cannot solve the problem. Even if you find you cannot do or say anything right now, it's important to recognize that bullying is wrong.
>
> Rather than deciding there is something wrong with you, concentrate on developing yourself so that you can effect a positive change in the future. If you end up in a fight and only get beaten up yourself, it won't solve anything. You have to find a long-term solution.
>
> Basically, unless we cultivate an awareness of human rights in society, we cannot begin to prevent abuse. I hope that each of you will be aware of your own and others' rights, so that Japan can become an

ideal nation in its respect for human rights (Ibid., 123–124; see also Ikeda 2000, 148).

In his response, Ikeda encourages students in the Soka schools he founded to resolve problems wholly through dialogue and with concern for one's own and the others' humanity, or what is called their greater selves.

In yet another dialogue with youth, this time with leaders from the SGI-USA youth and student divisions, Ikeda's young interlocutors raise the topic of violence in school, contextualizing their question in the then recent shooting at Columbine High School in Colorado, and lamenting that some youth engage in and boast about violent behavior. Ikeda tells them:

> Nothing pains and saddens me more than to see young people – who possess such infinite potential for the future – physically harming and killing one another. When I was around the same age as those who are in the high school division now, I lost my eldest brother in World War II. He was a kind and gentle person.

> (...) Violence is an absolute evil. You lose if you resort to violence, regardless of the reason. You may think you have beaten your opponent, but ultimately you have lost. For when you harm another, you actually harm yourself. When it comes down to it, people who readily use violence and have no respect for others' lives have no respect for their own lives (Ikeda 2010a, 406).

Ikeda concludes, "The essence of violence is cowardice. It is because they are cowardly that people rely on brute force. They lack courage to pursue dialogue (...) A willingness to engage in dialogue is a sign of a thinking person" (Ibid.).

For me, the above exchanges are the most poignant moments in Ikeda's dialogues with young people. Whereas the topics discussed with world educators seem obvious if philosophical, the question and answer, raised by students, reifies the immediacy of bullying in their lives and thereby highlights the reason Ikeda focuses on bullying so intently in his dialogues with youth and world educators. In other words, it is through such immediate issues as bullying – and ending bullying through dialogic becoming – that Ikeda sees the larger, aforementioned philosophical goals of peaceful coexistence being achieved.

Conclusion

In this chapter I have attempted to examine Ikeda's philosophy and practice of dialogue *on* education, *in* education and *as* education for peace and social policy. I have done so by excerpting passages from his dialogues with world educators and with students enrolled at the Soka schools he founded. Considering these broadly through a Bakhtinian lens of dialogism, I believe Ikeda's cross-cultural dialogues on education reveal his firm belief that dialogue is not only a forum for discussing education for peace and social policy, but also, as for Bakhtin, it is the most educative means for fully realizing our deepest humanity. Ikeda asserts, "I can not emphasize enough the importance of dialogue, for I believe that the propensity for logic and discussion is the proof of one's humanity. In other words, only when we are immersed in an ocean of language do we become truly human" (Ikeda 1999, 182). Thus, for Ikeda dialogue *is* education and education is dialogic becoming.

CHAPTER 6

Daisaku Ikeda and Innovative Education

Wayne Hudson

Characteristics of Ikeda's dialogical approach

Daisaku Ikeda has engaged in dialogue with a very wide range of people, including Arnold Toynbee, André Malraux, Bryan Wilson, Linus Pauling, Johan Galtung, Mikhail Gorbachev, Elise Boulding, Majid Tehranian, Tu Weiming, Hazel Henderson and Harvey Cox.[1] In all his dialogues he seeks to promote not only compassion, peace and understanding but a sense of possible *convergence* between people from different cultures, speaking different languages, and inhabiting different symbolic universes. Although he may seem to be dialoguing with people of different religions or none at all, in fact Ikeda is always dialoguing with human beings about the one reality, on which they have different windows. In his dialogues he assumes that the particularities of different religions and traditions are to a considerable degree cultural and historical. That is, they do not go directly to the nature of the truth itself. Nor do they go directly to the nature of the universe in which we live. There is also often a restrained and discreet *postreligious impulse* operating in his texts: a reverence for traditional formulations and ideas, allied to a tendency not to treat them as the only way in which the truth could be expressed, especially in the future. Thus in a recent dialogue Ikeda comments:

We have taken our stand for a religious renaissance with the happiness of the ordinary people as its goal. We strive to determine the nature of religion for a new age that will enable people to live in such a way as to manifest their true humanity.

We also want to discover ways in which religion can contribute to human happiness and social development (Ikeda and Cox 2009a, 35).

In dialogue after dialogue Ikeda opens the way for future syntheses in which partial and currently divergent perspectives could be reconciled. In Ikeda's dialogues there is no aggressive assertion *against* traditional Buddhism, Christianity, Confucianism, Hinduism, Daoism, or even atheism. However, there are gentle hints that in the future *a certain humanization of the historical religions might occur.*[2] There are also suggestions that this humanization could eventually link up with *a phenomenologically sensitive qualitative cosmology* which, while it would certainly not displace the instrumental sciences on which the success of techno-scientific societies depend, would allow *a greater space for the spiritual intuitions of humanity* and *a basis for mutual understanding across traditional cultural and religious divides.*

Consider the following passages, selected from among hundreds of pages of texts affirming a postreligious stance. First in Ikeda's dialogue with British pioneer of the sociology of religion, Bryan Wilson:

Belief in and respect (even aspiration) for something that cannot be directly perceived through the senses assists human beings in controlling and sublimating their desires and anxieties. As long as no drastic changes occur in human nature or the general situation in which man finds himself, I believe the emergence of religious emotion to be both inevitable and essential (Ikeda and Wilson 1984, 5).

In his exchanges with Turkish social anthropologist Nur Yalman Ikeda noted: "The role of religion is not to restrict human beings but to liberate them and turn them towards self-realization. What the twenty-first century needs is religion for the sake of humanity and the ordinary people – not religion for its own sake" (Ikeda and Yalman 2009b, 15). Talking about global challenges such as nuclear weapons proliferation, global warming and poverty in his preface to the same volume, Ikeda wrote: "They must be confronted through the power of dialogue and education, designed to unite the hearts of all individuals. The time has come for a united effort by all humanity – an effort that must transcend all differences of race and nationality, religion and culture" (Ibid., xi).

This exchange, from Ikeda's dialogue with Iranian-born international communications expert Majid Tehranian, is especially significant:

> **Ikeda:** "Difference" can mean "diversity." Similarities provide a basis for cooperation, but we must also be aware of our differences, ready to respect each religion's role and the strengths of the other. Then we will find ways we can each contribute to the world." (...) A Buddha does not just sit idly in meditation but walks among the masses, telling them about the way of happiness.

> **Tehranian:** What you say reminds me of a Sufi poem written by Sa'adi, a great 13th-century Persian poet: "To pray is nothing but serving humanity. Prayer rugs, rosaries, and begging bowls are but vanity" (Ikeda and Tehranian 2003, 25).

> **Ikeda:** I can see your point very well. Dogma represents the state of being bound up in the narrow, petty fetters of the ego. By working for the benefit of humanity and by serving people, we can free ourselves from such fetters (Ibid., 28–29).

One last example can be found in the joint preface Ikeda wrote with Mikhail Gorbachev:

> Our philosophies and articles of faith differ. One author was the last secretary general of the Communist Party of the Soviet Union. The other is the leader of the largest religious movement in Japan. For us to find a common spiritual basis enabling us to sit down at the discussion table and discover shared points through which we can understand the outstanding events of the 20th century has two consequences. First, it shows the significance of human experiences

in the 20th century. Second, it proves that everyone living today –
including the two of us, born and raised in different circumstances
– has much in common (Ikeda and Gorbachev 2005, vii).

These little-noted features of dialogue Ikeda-style matter in a world in which
peoples of every kind are increasingly coming together. This is especially so
because Ikeda's approach has *a universal cognitional basis in operations which
human beings from all cultures can perform*. Thus in his dialogue with Harvey
Cox Ikeda declares:

> The best dialogue requires informality and openness. Effective, lively
> and warm, mind-to-mind exchanges are of the utmost importance.
> We need to stress our shared humanity. We must realize that people
> of different races and cultural backgrounds have beloved family and
> friends, and that they experience the same joys and sorrows that we
> experience (Ikeda and Cox 2009a, 9).

This is a crucial aspect of Ikeda's achievement, more explicit in his pro-
nouncements of recent years, but always implicitly there – both in his love
of literature from every part of the world and in his personal photography.
Confronted with photography of the magnificent sky, human beings from all
over the world react in highly predictable, although culturally different ways.
In many cases they recognize a transreality which traverses their different
culturally formed experiences. This matrix of universal anthropology and a
qualitative phenomenology of nature underlies Ikeda's discussion of many
points of divergence and allows him to plumb for the real meanings others
attach to their doctrines and symbols. In this way, Ikeda is able to follow
a "two minds in dialogue" format, while also working towards something
else: *a new level of shared meaning in which different traditions will find their place*,
transcended in some of their characteristics, but in no sense negated. Indeed,
Ikeda in dialogue practices with supreme tact what the German philosopher
Georg Wilhelm Friedrich Hegel called *Aufhebung*. This is the key term in
Hegel's philosophy. It is standardly translated by the neologism "sublation."
However, it really means a movement in which contents are transcended, such
that the positive features are realized at a higher level, while the negative
features are overcome. Ikeda's dialogues point towards a future transcendence

of particular spiritual traditions in this sense. Here I differ with Obelleiro's emphasis on the inevitability of differences in chapter 3 of this volume.

Expanding inclusivist, correlationist and convergentist features

Having identified these characteristics of Ikeda's approach to dialogue, I now suggest that it is possible to design pedagogies that extend Ikeda's inclusivist, correlationist and convergentist approach to dialogue in courses which embody untraditional avant-garde pedagogic design. In the remainder of this chapter I discuss two examples of education of this kind that are of some importance for peace.

First, consider *the case of education for global citizenship*. Although there is increasing worldwide interest in global citizenship, not enough has yet been done to develop forms of pedagogy and ways of teaching to equip young people to be global citizens. Yet the horizon of global citizenship will almost certainly transform schools and universities in both predictable and unpredictable ways in the near future.

Education for global citizenship attempts to strengthen and enhance the respect and sense of shared species identity which human beings feel for one another. It encourages the formation of new global ethical values and familiarizes students with them in ways which do not undermine or threaten their existing national, cultural, or religious identities. To achieve this, education for global citizenship teaches students to think about existing subject matter in global ways. For example, history, philosophy, art and religion can all be taught on a world scale and in a way that emphasizes interconnections between different parts of the world. In the longer term, education for global citizenship should include specific information about such matters as global institutions, world religion, and world law. In the short term, however, effective education for global citizenship can take the form of *short immersion courses* which extend the interests and capacities of staff and students. I have myself developed and taught courses of this kind.

One immersion course which can be used to promote global citizenship is an innovative course in world history (excluding Europe and the Americas) up to 1400. The course is entitled *World History Made Graphic*. It has a number of unusual features:

1. Unlike standard British or American world history courses, it is not information-based and makes no serious attempt to teach any part of history in detail. On the contrary, it omits references to dates, battles and kings, except where these are introduced for indicative purposes.

2. Instead, it has *a theoretical basis in evolutionary theory* and in the form of *historical sociology* called organizational materialism associated with the work of Michael Mann, both of which ground the course's privileging of material factors. This immersion course integrates history with the natural sciences and students are taught to think about historical data in terms of *a calculus of probabilities*. In effect, they are encouraged to predict what happened and where, and use is made of virtual worlds and other non-traditional resources.

3. The course also breaks with all forms of history inspired by historicism and promotes a radically non-Eurocentric and non-teleological reading of the historical record. It also subverts romantic and modernist understandings of world history, based on celebration of uniqueness, difference and dialectical contrast logics.

4. For the purposes of an introductory course, this immersion course privileges *geography* over contingent fact and *structural patterns* over historical detail.

5. The course is also highly visual and privileges the use of *simplified graphics* as opposed to maps. Unlike maps, graphics are easy to understand, but not necessarily strictly accurate from either a geographical or historical point of view. The graphics are supported and supplemented by the use of concept cards, icons, factor sheets and core data sheets.

6. Students are also asked to actively debate different interpretations of the course materials in small groups.

The core of the pedagogy is that it takes the students over the macro-historical record very quickly and inculcates a powerful sense of recurrent patterns. It is inspiring and exciting, and all cohorts with whom it has been tested have been enthusiastic, even though many of them had never studied history before, or had mainly natural science backgrounds. The course takes only 14 hours and can be given over a single weekend. The evidence suggests that students' interpretative skills are enhanced by the pedagogy in a cumulatively empowering way.

Another immersion course I have designed to promote global citizenship teaches students to think about historical problems in context-free ways and emphasizes the contemporary potential of the materials discussed, not only what they meant in their historical context. This course is more radical in educational terms and lends itself to realizations in computer-assisted learning and hypermedia. It is informed by the latest international literature on constructivist educational methods. This course teaches students concept construction and data processing as forms of deep learning without involving them in traditional studies of historical context. It can be delivered in a computer-assisted high-technology format using hyper-media such as interactive CD laser discs.

The pedagogy used in both courses is informed by the international literature on constructivism, especially by the work on instructional design by the Cognition and Technology group at Vanderbilt University. Constructivists assume that experiences are central to learning, and that students construct their knowledge on the basis of their experience. They further hypothesize that learning outcomes depend on how learners construct their knowledges and that reflection on constructed meaning promotes further meaning. A constructivist pedagogy provides the student with *experience of knowledge construction processes*. Students experience the need for *multiple perspectives*; they are also required to evaluate *alternative solutions to problems*. Constructivist strategies impact upon both knowledge construction and the way in which learning is conceived.

Despite their complex background, however, the success of these courses lies in their simplicity and their transversal range. The students find that their existing knowledge is extended and galvanized by these courses. They also grasp the ethical shift involved in considering the mega-picture and human experiences across many cultures.

Obviously education for global citizenship will need to take different forms in different countries and any immersion course would need to be redesigned to meet the needs of a particular culture and language. Here, however, I emphasize that these courses extend Daisaku Ikeda's convergentist methodology of dialogue. They have a universal cognitional basis in operations which human beings from all cultures can perform and teach students to perform these operations in a systematic and structured way. This produces emergent awareness of recurrent patterns and intrinsic intelligibilities across a vast range of historical data. It also contributes to a global historical mentality which enables learners to think with and beyond traditional spiritual traditions towards a common postreligious future.

Second, consider *the case of multifaith dialogue,* which has assumed great importance for peace in the contemporary world; especially dialogue between Christians and Muslims and Muslims and Hindus. A standard approach to multifaith dialogue assumes that: (1) there are religions; (2) the core of religions consists in beliefs; (3) these beliefs differ; and (4) it is desirable for believers in different religions to dialogue about their beliefs. This is roughly the standard model.

This model might be flawed to the extent that the best contemporary scholarship contests the notion that there are "religions," and also the notion that the core of "religions" consists in beliefs. In the scholarly literature religion is still commonly defined in terms of belief in and reverence for divine ruling powers, which may or may not be supernatural beings; an overwhelming experience of the holy, the sacred, awe, dread and a system of beliefs, practices, symbols, and ritual actions relating to super-human beings or powers beyond our knowledge and control. However, there is now considerable evidence that this is a nineteenth-century European pattern of interpretation which seriously distorts the historical record.[3]

Instead, what is needed now is *a disaggregated approach to the heterogeneous materials associated with "religion."* This approach avoids confusing "religion" with a single generic type. It recognizes that "religion" can often be analyzed into *historically changing ensembles of heterogeneous performances,* not all of which are spiritual or moral.

In the light of these considerations I now suggest that the standard approach to multifaith dialogue can be supplemented by a cognitive process approach exemplified in innovative pedagogy. A cognitive process approach implies that *it may sometimes be a mistake to take religious differences, especially differences of belief, as basic to dialogue and cooperation between spiritual traditions.* This view is consistent with recent research into the history of the concept of "religion," which shows that it is a European invention of recent date wrongly imposed on the rest of the world (Asad 1993). Instead, multifaith dialogue can take the form of *process in which members of different faith traditions participate.* As an alternative to dialogue about beliefs or sacred texts, a cognitive process approach is designed to heighten participants' awareness of the universal cognitive processing involved in the operations involved in appropriating radically different spiritual traditions.

The aim is to move multifaith dialogue beyond the impasse which affects attempts to bring faith traditions together, by promoting common participation in cognitive process. A cognitive process approach aims to expose participants to cognitive materials which they process together so that new cognitive positions and vocabularies emerge. Disagreements remain, but they are no longer seen as a problem. Instead, an historical shift is made towards a religious citizenship perspective, in which people from different faith traditions expand their sense and practice of their own duties. The goal of this kind of multifaith dialogue is not to celebrate *a separated pluralism*, but to encourage solidaristic mutual cooperation and respect across spiritual traditions.

To the extent that a pedagogy is made available which teaches participants to recognize the same or related cognitive operations in culturally divergent materials, a cognitive process approach may be more productive than attempts to "find the common ground" or dialogues about different doctrines, rituals, or symbols. Once participants have recognized universal cognitive operations in different spiritual traditions, multifaith dialogue can rise to an entirely different level and participants from different spiritual traditions can be asked to rethink historically variable definitions of religion, to develop a theory of religious citizenship applicable to spiritual traditions other than their own, and to construct prospections about possible spiritual futures.

A pedagogy of this type will raise the level of cognitive reflexivity achieved by participants and so open the way for a fair and unprejudiced consideration of possible postreligious futures. In this way, significantly new light is also thrown on the problem of postreligious emergence which now confronts all the major spiritual traditions – Indigenous, Hindu, Buddhist, Daoist, Jewish, Christian, and Islamic.

Once again I have developed pedagogy which can facilitate a cognitive process of this kind, including an immersion course on *World Philosophy Made Dramatic* and an immersion course on *Spirituality, Science and the Arts*. Recent developments in cognitive science provide the background to this pedagogy,[4] but again no knowledge of this background is required by participants and the materials used are simple. Here I give three examples of instructional materials used, before relating a cognitive process back to the dialogue methodology of Daisaku Ikeda.

Projective Figure 1

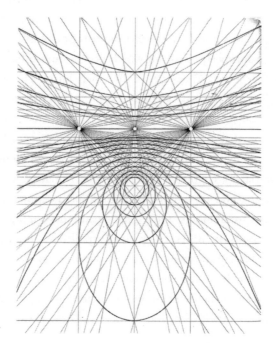

Projective geometry is unlike Euclidean geometry in that it is not a geometry of created forms, but of the relationships between form-creating entities:

namely points, lines and planes, which are defined in terms of one another. Figure 1 shows a family of curves constructed from lines that are projected from three points along a central line or horizon. Note that the tangents to the curves are given by the points at which the projected lines intersect (diagram from Whicher 1971, 174).

Projective Figure 2

Figure 2 shows another sequence of related curves without the projected lines that form the tangents to the created curves. The point of origin of the projected lines or rays of this figure is infinitely distant, whereas in the previous figure these points were fixed on the line of horizon (diagram from Whicher 1971, 166).

Projective Figures 3a and 3b

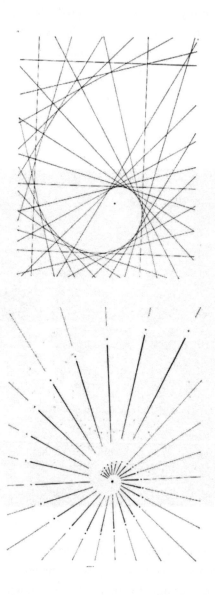

Figure 3a and 3b demonstrate the relationships between points and lines in the plane with respect to a single "circle-curve." Note again the reciprocal relationship between points and lines as they define the tangents to the curve. This relationship is expressed in a different manner in the bottom figure by removing the tangent lines. The presence of the circle-curve foregrounds the manner in which a point can be defined as a manifold of all the lines it contains, just as the line is a manifold of all the points it contains (diagram from Whicher 1971, 187).

Each of these figures can be worked through with participants from different spiritual traditions. In each case it is possible to make the participants aware of the cognitive operations involved in interpreting the figures, and in each case it is possible to relate the figure to well-known spiritual traditions. In this way the participants can be helped to see that they recognize and understand the cognitive operational dimension of the particular tradition which they previously understood as alien and excluded from their own spiritual understanding. Thus the first figure can be used to establish that the interactivity between different planes and worlds which is basic to Hinduism and to some forms of Mahayana Buddhism involves universal operations with which Christians, Jews, and Muslims are also familiar. The second figure can be used to lead participants to the insight that the duality which is fundamental to Zoroastrianism and Daoism is involved in the ordinary cognition of other spiritual traditions. The third (double) figure can be used to familiarize participants with the possibility that the incarnation of the infinite which is central to Christianity has a universal basis in our cognitive operations. In all three cases there is no suggestion that recognizing universal cognitive operations leads participants to adopt spiritual traditions other than their own. However, such pedagogy does raise the level of inquiry and helps participants to see that the crucial question is how we should deploy our universal cognitive operations in a globalizing and complex world.

A cognitive process approach to multifaith dialogue does not lead to a monist dissolution of profound differences, or to motherhood-type amalgamations of the world's spiritual traditions. Differences are not overcome, but they are placed within cognitive contexts which allow transitivity across spiritual traditions. On the other hand, it is not difficult to see that a cognitive process approach has a convergentist character and, moreover, one that leads fairly quickly to engagement with the emergence in all traditions of a postreligious horizon. The results are likely to be favorable to religious peace, but they also open up forms of cognitive emergence which may not leave spiritual traditions unchanged.

Conclusion

Daisaku Ikeda's contributions to contemporary Buddhism are well known, but the wider implications of his legacy remain to be explored. In this chapter I have suggested that his *inclusive, correlationist* and *convergentist* approach to dialogue can be continued and extended in the area of innovative education in ways that do not depend upon his own considerable mastery of a range of Buddhist and European high cultural texts. In so far as this is the case, Ikeda may have more to contribute than most of his followers currently suggest.

PART IV

DIALOGUE ON GLOBAL ISSUES

Chapter 7

Dialogical Approaches of Daisaku Ikeda and South–South Network

Christine Atieno

There is no true joy in a life lived closed up in the little shell of the self.
When you take one step to reach out to people, when you meet with others
and share their thoughts and sufferings, infinite compassion and wisdom
well up within your heart. Your life is transformed.

Genuine dialogue is a ceaseless and profound spiritual exertion that seeks
to effect a fundamental human transformation in both ourselves and others.
Dialogue challenges us to confront and transform the destructive impulses
inherent in human life. I earnestly believe that the energy generated by this
courageous effort can break the chains of resignation and apathy that bind the
human heart, unleashing renewed confidence and vision for the future.

We are not born human in any but a biological sense; it is only by
immersion in the "ocean of language and dialogue" fed by the springs of
cultural tradition that we can learn to know ourselves and others and thus
learn the ways of being human.

(Ikeda 2012a)

Introduction

Some of the approaches of both Daisaku Ikeda and the South–South Network
(SSN) have been embraced – and some others need to be further explored – by

those who seek amicable and fair settlements to conflicts within the southern hemisphere through the use of the dialogue mechanism. In this chapter I attempt to formulate new strategies/approaches/mechanisms on how the principles and/ or practices mentioned may be further explored as dialogue tools or techniques for solving conflict within respective societies in the Global South and on a global scale. Once we recognize our shared humanity regardless of aspects such as location or religion, we become aware that we are interrelated and interconnected in one way or another and that all humans have creative potentials to resolve conflicts which can be realized through a participatory approach based on constructive dialoguing, shared cultures, and historical and geographical backgrounds. Thus in this chapter I also embark on a brief comparative analysis of the principles and/or practices adopted by the institutions Mr. Ikeda has founded, and which he represents, and those of the South–South Network, in order to identify points of thought and equilibrium and their implications that could further enhance dialogue amongst armed groups and other parties in conflicts.

The South–South Network has adopted a Southern perspective in its approaches in seeking remedies to conflicts. It is a tricontinental-anchored initiative, from the global South (i.e. Asia, Africa and Latin America) which seeks to develop more effective approaches, instruments and intellectual resources for the constructive engagement of non-state armed groups (NSAGs). The term "Southern," here, is in reference to the shared similarities of internal/intra-state armed conflicts in Africa, Asia and Latin America – regions which also share a history of colonialism and post-colonialism. The South–South Network seeks in its international activities to secure relations of *equality* and *co-responsibility* in the true spirit and relations of *internationalism*.

SSN's organizational configuration and organizational culture incorporates *inter-regional and intra-regional* networks of mainly people's and non-governmental organizations and field practitioners as well as academic, research and policy institutions and workers.

The Network serves as a *specialist* vehicle to support Southern and internationalist efforts to *constructively* engage NSAGs in the areas of human rights (HR), international humanitarian law (IHL), conflict resolution, peacebuilding, human security, human development, democratization and good governance, including "non-state governance."

The rationale for SSN's work is that NSAGs affect the lives of people for better or for worse, especially in situations of armed conflict and insurgent transitions (e.g. from war to peace, from authoritarianism to democracy). NSAGs have become the dominant face of modern warfare and now have a central role in contemporary armed conflict. Some of them have already emerged as global actors and they are increasingly becoming subjects of international law. The greater the threat of NSAGs to human security and to innocent civilians, the greater the need for humanitarian and other forms of engagement with these NSAGs, irrespective of their location.

Daisaku Ikeda, on the other hand, is a philosopher and educationist who represents institutions whose objectives are in pursuit of restoring broken inter-state/ interpersonal relationships through a philosophy centered on dialogue. Notably, his remedies to regional/international conflicts are directed towards dialogue and the transformation of our inner lives. Ikeda's approaches are a reflection of principles and values inspired by Buddhist spirituality – shared in a secular way – entailing *inner transformation*, *dialogue* and *global citizenship*, which he strongly believes are components of a way of life. His Buddhist principles and practices have enabled him to integrate the various aspects of his life, i.e. his faith, work, academic life, and sense of social responsibility. His belief in dialogue is based on a deep faith in humanity and a pragmatic recognition of the inability of violence to produce lasting positive change. It is his belief that each individual has a potential that needs to be brought out through appropriate methods, with dialogue being one of these methods, and he thus encourages person-to-person exchanges. Ikeda stresses the importance of believing in oneself and in the unique abilities each individual possesses. Accordingly, and I agree with Ikeda, no matter how complex global challenges may seem, we must remember that it is we ourselves who have given rise to them. It is therefore impossible that they would be beyond our power as human beings to resolve.

Inner transformation allows for better dialogue and greater capacity for global citizenship; dialogue encourages inner transformation and polishes one's identity as a global citizen, and attempts to become a global citizen necessitate inner transformation and dialogue. Ikeda's main sources of inspiration were his war memories, his mentor Josei Toda, and a desire to serve humanity (Urbain 2010).

Some concepts concerning a Philosophy of Peace

As a pragmatic conflict mediation approach, dialogue presents a real challenge as a tool for achieving peace. This can be attributed to the fact that during mediation processes parties at war often have positioned attitudes and probably preconceived perceptions that the processes will not work in their favor. This has proved not to be the case, as compromises have to be reached through the rationality and wisdom of both the mediators and the aggrieved.

With a focus on the conflicts in Africa and Asia, especially those involving armed groups, we have to take note of the religious element that characterizes some of these instances of civil strife. For example, the Sudan Peace Process, through the discussions on the right of self-determination, led to the signing of the "Machakos Protocol" in July 2002. In the case of Southeast Asia, with a specific focus on the Mindanao/Philippines Peace Process, the negotiations between the Government of the Republic of the Philippines (GRP) and the Moro Islamic Liberation Front (MILF) have an element of the religious factor, due to the fact that a majority of the Moros are Muslims by faith.

Emphasis should be placed on the importance of understanding that within the various religions that are practiced: Buddhism, Christianity, Islam, and others, there exist aspects highlighting or defining peace, which to an extent also mention inter/intra-relationships especially concerning how human beings should coexist peacefully amongst themselves and co-relate positively with their surrounding environment. Religious components should therefore not be sidelined during peace negotiations as they play a vital role in understanding the other parties' thinking. This is not to state that a lot of emphasis should be placed on the religious factor, but rather to stress that within the specific contexts of these three most practiced religions there exist texts relating to the search for inner peace. It is important for this element to be factored in by mediators during peace negotiations and reflected in the final agreements.

It is my belief and principle that for one to give peace to others, one must start with the self. As an individual, one has to be at peace with the inner self in order to share with others. The principles and practices of inner transformation[1] are to an extent engrained in our various religious upbringings, often underlying – and mixed with – other cultural and traditional norms.

Relating this to international peacebuilding, the point to be fathomed here, while making various comparisons between inter-religious understandings on peace, is to ascertain the interconnectedness of humans despite their various religious practices and beliefs. By interconnectedness I simply mean the ability of an individual or members of panels on peace negotiations, including the armed group's representatives, during deliberations, to empathize impartiality, irrespective of their religious views or practices. In addition, it reflects on the interconnections of religions or philosophies in championing concepts of peace in their scriptures and writings. This is to say, the "tied-in" factor that shows that a Buddhist can relate to a Christian who in turn can relate to a Hindu, a Muslim, an atheist and so on. One element that many religions and philosophies have in common is an emphasis on inner peace and a conviction that it can be achieved.

Inner peace: some examples

Buddhism is one of the world's oldest religions and at its core is the quest to understand life and to help people overcome their basic suffering. Buddhism asserts that all humans have particular life-tendencies around which their emotions, thoughts and activities usually center and to which they tend to revert when external stimuli arise. The practice guides individuals on the best ways to live amongst one another. A peace verse attributed to the Buddha in *The Dhammapada* teaches: "He who is tranquil in body, tranquil in speech, tranquil in mind, who is well integrated, and who is unattached to worldly things – such a person is said to be at peace" (Sangharakshita 2001). The principle of cause and effect suggests we can change our destiny, which we may have thought unchangeable. This is the hope and promise offered by Buddhist practice. Buddha means "awakened one," and the historical Buddha (Shakyamuni or Siddhartha Gautama) discovered that all humans have a potential for enlightenment in the depths of their lives (SGI-USA 1998). In Nichiren Buddhism, all Ten Worlds – hell, hunger, anger, animality, humanity, heaven, learning, realization, bodhisattva and buddhahood – are viewed as conditions of life that all people have the potential to experience. At any moment, one of the ten will manifest while the other nine remain dormant, but there is always the potential for change. Ikeda wrote:

Peace is a competition between despair and hope, between dis-
empowerment and committed persistence. To the degree that
powerlessness takes root in people's consciousness, there is a great
tendency to resort to force. Powerlessness breeds violence (Ikeda
2006).

Along the same lines, Krishnamurti said:

The man who carries a gun does not solve the problem, he only
increases the problem; for each war produces another war, it is an
historical fact. It is important to understand yourself, your conditioning, your upbringing, the way you are educated; because, the
government, the whole system, is your own projection. The world
is you, the world is not separate from you; the world with its problems is projected out of your responses, out of your reactions, so the
solution does not lie in creating further reactions. Peace is not the
denial of war; it is not a theory, not an ideal to be achieved after
ten incarnations, ten years or ten days. As long as the mind has
not understood its own activity, it will create more misery; and the
understanding of the mind is the beginning of peace (Krishnamurti
1950).

Muslims use the greeting "*As-Salaamu alaykum*," which can be translated as
"Peace be upon you." To me, this means that in Islam, before dialogue can
begin, the blessing "peace be upon you" is bestowed and wished upon the
other party. The aim of this is for the inner self of each person to remain
solemn so that understanding and rationality may be reached and used
amongst the discussants.

The Quran turns our attention to the high value of human life, whether it
is that of a Muslim or non-Muslim, and makes it absolutely forbidden to take
an innocent life unjustly. The gravity of such a crime is equated, in the Quran,
with the killing of all humanity.

On that account: We ordained for the Children of Israel that if
any one slew a person – unless it be for murder or for spreading

mischief in the land – it would be as if he slew the whole people: and if any one saved a life, it would be as if he saved the life of the whole people. Then although there came to them Our apostles with clear Signs, yet, even after that, many of them continued to commit excesses in the land (5:32).

In the following passage, inner tranquility is said to contribute to good health:

Some of the most revered scholars would recite the Quranic verses that speak about tranquility during times of disturbance, and this proved to have a great effect. Ibn Al-Qayyim said in his book *Madaarij As-Saalikeen*, "Whenever Shaykhul-Islam Ibn Taymiyyah found things difficult, he would recite the verses mentioning tranquility. I heard him say about a difficult situation that happened to him during his sickness, 'When I got very sick, I asked those who were around me to recite on me the verses that speak about tranquility. Once they did, I recovered completely'" (Islamweb 2012).

Christianity too has several verses in the Holy Scriptures which highlight issues pertaining to inner peace. These can be found in the books of Matthew, Colossians, Philippians and John. The latter summarizes it well: "Jesus said, 'Peace I leave with you. My peace I give unto you: not as the world giveth, give I unto you. Let not your heart be troubled, neither let it be afraid'" (African New Testament 2004).

During turmoil and when facing a crisis, practicing Christians may seek inner strength and peace by referring to the biblical verses aligned to the sufferings in the book of Psalms 121:1–2; 7–8, which state, "I will lift my eyes to the hills – from whence comes my help? My help comes from the Lord, who made heaven and earth; (...) the Lord shall preserve you from all evil; He shall preserve your soul; the Lord shall preserve your going out and your coming in from this time forth, and even forevermore." Other biblical verses that refer to the importance of seeking inner peace include John (16:33) which states, "These things I have spoken to you, that in Me you may have peace. In the world you will have tribulation; but be of good cheer, I have overcome the world." Philippians (4:6,7) states: "Be anxious for nothing, but in everything by prayer and supplication, with thanksgiving, let your requests be made known to God; And the peace of God, which surpasses all understanding, will guard your hearts and minds through Christ Jesus" (African New Testament 2004).

Peace agreements and negotiations through the dialogue mechanism

One principle that leaders should pay attention to is that of the oneness of life and its environment, which is central to Nichiren Buddhism, and which describes the inseparable relationship between individuals and their surroundings. Essentially, our life is not confined to ourselves, but exerts an influence on our families, communities, nations, and ultimately all humanity (SGI-USA 1998).

Africa and Southeast Asia (SEA) have to face the reality that many countries are still far away from democracy and freedom. Most countries in SEA are facing the problems of "intra-state" conflict which in turn limits how and to what extent the Association of Southeast Asian Nations (ASEAN) can respond to domestic conflicts in the region. One example is the government of the Philippines, which has battled a series of insurgencies by groups such as the Moro National Liberation Front (MNLF) and the MILF in Mindanao while peace negotiations continue.

While focusing on the Security Sector Reform (SSR) process, external SSR advocates must first *establish trust with the local authority* and be sensitive to local wisdom. There is no quick-fix solution or one-size-fits-all approach.[2] An example of a resolution reached after a lengthy negotiation process in Southeast Asia is the establishment of the ASEAN Intergovernmental Commission on Human Rights (AICHR).

In August 2005, after several rounds of difficult negotiations, the government of Indonesia and the Free Aceh Movement (GAM) signed a Memorandum of Understanding, an agreement that transformed the war in Aceh into one of the success stories of civil war termination in recent times. As a result of a series of post-Memorandum of Understanding (MoU) negotiations between stakeholders, the Law on Governing Aceh (LoGA) was created.

In Africa, I briefly focus on the dialogue processes of two post-conflict country cases – those of Sierra Leone and Sudan – which led to the signing of comprehensive peace agreements.

The Sierra Leone Peace Process involved multiple negotiations between the government and the conflict actors – mainly the rebels – in order to restore relationships. Other players included international organizations, UN peacekeepers, returnees/marginalized people and also shadow rebels (Bashiru-Kargbo 2012).

On 7 July 1999, President Kabbah and Revolutionary United Front (RUF) leader Foday Sankoh signed the Lome Peace Accord in Togo's capital, which granted Sankoh a position in the transitional government as well as amnesty for him and all combatants, and also committed the signing parties to the disarmament, demobilization and reintegration (DDR) program; that is, the demobilization and disarmament of combatants and their reintegration into civil society.

The dialogue element is found in the preamble of the accord: "Recalling earlier initiatives undertaken by the countries of the sub-region and the International Community, aimed at bringing about a negotiated settlement of the conflict in Sierra Leone, and culminating in the Abidjan Peace Agreement of 30 November, 1996 and the Economic Community of West African States (ECOWAS) Peace Plan of 23 October, 1997." This dialogue process was based on mediated conversations between the Government of the Republic of Sierra Leone (GoSL) and RUF rebels under the auspices of the chairperson of ECOWAS.

In November 2000, the government and the RUF signed the Abuja Ceasefire Agreement in Nigeria, which included provisions for a ceasefire, disarmament, and deployment of United Nations Mission in Sierra Leone (UNAMSIL) peacekeepers in parts of the country under RUF control. On 16 January 2002, the UN and the government of Sierra Leone signed an agreement establishing the Special Court for Sierra Leone in Freetown to "try those who bear the greatest responsibility for serious violations of international humanitarian law and Sierra Leonean law committed in the territory of Sierra Leone since 30 November 1996" (Special Court 2002). The aftermath of the dialogue process in the Sierra Leone conflict saw the signing of several accords, from the Lome Peace Accord to the Abidjan Peace Accord and finally to the setting up of the UNAMSIL SCSL that has since sustained peace in the country.

Recently in Sudan, the Doha Document for Peace in Darfur (DDPD) signed in mid-2011 between the Government of Sudan (GoS) and Darfur armed groups, recognizes that "the Darfur conflict cannot be resolved militarily and a durable solution can only be obtained through an inclusive political process." The instrument further recognizes "religion, beliefs, traditions and customs as sources of moral strength and inspiration for the Sudanese people" (Doha Document 2011). My interpretation of these clauses would be that despite the conflicting parties signing the peace agreement, there has to be a continuous dialogue amongst those seeking political leadership/office in order to resolve differences that may constantly arise during the implementation of the agreement.

The Comprehensive Peace Agreement (CPA) signed in 2005 between the GoS and the Sudan People's Liberation Movement/Army (SPLM/A), recognizes the principle of dialogue reflected in the element of "negotiation" in its Preambles, Principles and the Transition Process as well as its Agreed Principles of the Machakos Protocol. They state: "the parties – GoS and SPLM/A – are committed to a negotiated, peaceful, comprehensive resolution to the conflict; [and to] Negotiate and implement a comprehensive ceasefire to end the suffering and killing of the Sudanese people" (Comprehensive Agreement 2005).

In my view, establishing trust and involvement in a negotiation process is a chain of continuous dialoguing and communication engagement amongst the authorities – whether political or civilian – with the end result of understanding one another and deriving amicable solutions. Many of the peace agreements signed provide frameworks to address post-conflict development. In all, dialogue remains a key principle engrained in these instruments.

Dialogical approaches of Daisaku Ikeda and the South–South Network

Ikeda is guided by the teachings of Nichiren Buddhism, which encourage practitioners to repay the "four debts of gratitude." The debts of gratitude include those owed to all living beings, one's father and mother, one's sovereign, and the three treasures of Buddhism (Ikeda 2012b). Always keeping in mind the many persecutions his mentor Josei Toda underwent at the hand of the wartime Japanese military authorities, Ikeda is filled with determination to avoid state-sponsored or any other kind of violence, to mend relations amongst states and communities – both local and international – guided by the spirit of reducing tension and suffering. As a principle that enables people to elevate their spirituality, the four debts of gratitude can be linked to the biblical verses of the beatitudes in Christianity, to the Commandments of God and the general belief in a Supreme Being and the reliance on the latter for strength, guidance and protection in times of turmoil.

In his work, Ikeda often emphasizes interconnectedness and the fact that all human beings are part of a web of relationships. Our being is a part of human society and our lives depend upon and are subject to the welfare and misfortune of the family, community, nation and group to which we belong. In a dialogue between Ikeda and Joseph Rotblat, the following example sums up the two men's conviction in that principle.

> **Rotblat:** First of all, let me provide a general perspective on the meaning of "responsibility." By "responsibility," I am referring to the social responsibility held by all people, not only scientists. As members of society, each one of us belongs to some kind of group. In contemporary society, it is impossible for anyone to live a completely isolated life. Indeed, life as we know it is made possible by the assistance of others.

> **Ikeda:** I believe that this is called "interdependence." Our lives are made possible by the help and hard work of many people, including our forebears, whose legacy we enjoy. It is important for us humbly to acknowledge this reality. (...) In oriental culture, this notion is expressed in terms of "gratitude." (...) To forget one's debt to another is shameful (Rotblat and Ikeda 2007, 87–8).

Ikeda's philosophy

The effort to meet and speak with people has been a consistent focus of Ikeda's activities. He has built bridges of communication where walls of suspicion and mistrust have been erected. His *active compassion* for all human beings is one of the core attributes allowing him to take action for peace. In addition to this, he also lays emphasis on the qualities of *courage* and *wisdom* that are at the heart of the process of inner transformation. Amongst his beliefs is the conviction that relations between individual human beings are the foundation of relations between countries and that the construction of goodwill depends on bonds of trust and friendship. It is therefore important for people to work together to transform suspicion into trust, and fear into friendship.

> So long as human history continues, we will face the perennial challenge of realizing, maintaining and strengthening peace through dialogue, of making dialogue the sure and certain path to peace. We must uphold and proclaim this conviction without cease, whatever coldly knowing smiles or cynical critiques may greet us (Ikeda 2005).

An example of Ikeda's endeavors to build "bridges" for peace, already mentioned in chapter 2 of this volume, is in his contribution to the restoration of Sino–Japanese relations. In 1968, Japan and China were technically in a state of war and anti-Chinese and anticommunist sentiments were widespread in Japan. Ikeda then issued a proposal for the normalization of Japan–China relations. This action helped establish the groundwork for a series of political-level exchanges with China, culminating in restoration of diplomatic relations in 1972.

Ikeda's tools

Ikeda has long asserted that dialogue, in the form of open exchanges of ideas and perspectives, is the most certain way to build the foundations of peace. He emphasizes that the true value of dialogue is not to be found solely in the results it produces but also in the process of dialogue itself, as human spirits engage with and elevate each other to a higher realm.

Ikeda himself has learned a lot from one-on-one mentorship sessions with Josei Toda since August 1947. This spirit of dialogue and personal care is at the core of many of the institutions Ikeda has established. The Min-On Concert Association founded in 1963 – with the objective of promoting friendship and cultural exchanges through musical activities – and the Tokyo

Fuji Art Museum established in 1983, are examples of institutions founded in order to serve as dialogue channels, promoting understanding and trust through the arts.

Soka University was established in 1971 in Japan and in 1987 in the US. Over the years, the world has witnessed the expansion of Soka Gakkai's[3] overseas activities, with members as well as networks across more than 192 countries and territories. Soka Gakkai International (SGI) has actively promoted dialoguing with educators around the world through public lectures at various universities on all continents.

The establishment of research institutes such as the Institute of Oriental Philosophy, which actively engages in interfaith dialogue, the Ikeda Center for Peace, Learning and Dialogue, and the Toda Institute for Global Peace and Policy Research is also meant to promote communication at the global level.

Ikeda's achievements are the result of fierce struggles to overcome numerous challenges, and the process continues today as Ikeda keeps on developing a network of educational and academic exchanges and collaboration. Ikeda wrote:

> The most important question is what we dedicate our life to. The strength or weakness of our determination is what makes the difference between a life at the mercy of fate and a noble life shining with purpose (Ikeda 2009).

> When we wholeheartedly commit ourselves to "remembering" or retrieving that wish or vow from our subconscious mind and living an engaged and contributive life, we can tap previously unknown resources of wisdom, courage and compassion (*SGI Quarterly* 2009a).

The main purpose of the above brief review is to outline Ikeda's work and the institutions he has established in order to allow for a comparison with the South–South Network's activities.

SSN's approaches

SSN applies the principle of "Constructive Engagement" with non-state armed groups and surrounding communities involved, with the aim of

positively influencing NSAGs in so far as their operations affect the lives of
people and communities. The engagement process that SSN has adopted may
be summarized as:

- inclusive, participatory, dialogical and persuasive, rather than coercive
  and repressive;
- *not the following:* military engagement, law enforcement, criminal
  prosecution, economic sanctions and other "hard" policy instruments/
  measures against NSAGs *but rather:* SSN studies the implications of
  these on the overall effort of constructive engagement of NSAGs,
  including their legal accountability for international human rights
  law (IHRL) and international law of armed conflict/humanitarian law
  (ILAC/IHL) violations;
- focusing on the whole question of NSAG engagement, with the following priority areas or levels of engagement:

  1. Human Rights (HR), especially fundamental rights against
     torture, disappearances and displacement; IHL, especially basic
     protection from grave breaches; and accountability, both in its
     legal and non-legal/non-judicial forms

  2. peace processes, ceasefires, and other (human) security aspects,
     including disarmament, demobilization, reintegration and re-
     habilitation (DDRR) of combatants as well as their repatriation
     and resettlement and aspects of healing and reconciliation

  3. rehabilitation, reconstruction and development of conflict-affected
     areas, with priority to protection of refugees and internally dis-
     placed persons (IDPs)

  4. political democracy, including political and electoral reforms that
     would allow the viable transformation of NSAGs into political
     parties in a fair political system, and also good governance as
     applied to proto-state formations and post-conflict transition

  5. internal democracy (openness and tolerance, basic political and
     civil liberties) and other internal reforms, including struggles
     to deal with the corrupting influences of power, efforts to obtain
     gender equality, and many other endeavours (SSN 2012).

SSN's tools for dialoguing

Globalization has come to mean Western hegemony and dominance in the political, economic and cultural affairs of the world. This has also resulted in growing economic and social disparities between the Global North and Global South, as well as between the elites and the masses in both hemispheres. All these forms of hegemony, dominance and disparities have in turn generated various responses of social unrest, internal armed conflict and, most recently, global terrorism.

SSN's tools and approaches for dialoguing are similar to the previously discussed "peace agreements through dialogue." By and large, SSN – through direct engagement or mediated conversations – advocates for conflicts to be settled through the signing of well discussed and amicably settled declarations and comprehensive agreements.

This process entails direct and deliberate contact with NSAGs and encompasses the spectrum of communication activities, especially the classic acts of dialogue, negotiation, facilitation and mediation (Santos Jr. 2010).

Appendix 2 (see the end of the chapter, p. 136) briefly highlights some of SSN's approaches of complementing peace negotiations with the various dialogue mechanisms used, such as workshops, publications, etc. In summary: through its *Learning Exchange* activity, SSN and its networks have (co-) organized several international forums; through its *Direct Engagement* activity, SSN and its affiliates have been involved with various peace stakeholders, for instance in the Peace Processes of Sudan (SPLM/A) and Mindanao (MILF); through its *Research and Information Resource* activity, SSN and its affiliates continue to print publications and proceedings on organized workshops, field missions/research as well as published papers that directly or indirectly have influence on international policies; through its *Mechanism Development* activity, SSN has proposed supplementary legal instruments to be used while engaging the specific categories of NSAGs in peace processes; through its affiliates, signatures have been accorded by NSAGs in complying with the IHL norm on the stoppage of the use of landmines; and through its *Advocacy & Networking* activity, SSN has increased its affiliates at the global level since its inception in 2005.

It goes without saying that SSN has had its share of challenges during implementation of its various programs. Some of these, based on its tri-continental operations, include amongst others, logistics, communication and sponsorship problems which occasionally arise, thus hindering successful dialoguing with conflicting parties. Nonetheless, these have not deterred SSN from its commitment to achieve its global vision of uplifting humanity. This is to say that SSN continues to walk on the path of dialogue as it explores other channels with potential/strategic partners in order to fulfill its mission.

Brief comparative analysis of the principles and/or practices adopted by Ikeda and the South–South Network

In comparing Ikeda's and SSN's dialogical approaches, it can be noted that the former recommends spiritual engagement inspired by the practice of Nichiren Buddhism and translated into secular terms, while the latter's methods tend more towards the political aspects of engagement.

The emergence and disappearance of tranquility is governed by external circumstances. In this context, focusing on the armed conflicts in Africa and Asia, external circumstances could be categorized for example as use of small arms and light weapons (SALW) by armed groups, acts of terrorism, absence of transparent dialogue processes, and other negative elements. In a nutshell, they can be defined as a "breakdown in communication."

Ikeda's tools find their roots in the philosophy and practice of Buddhism, and as a result, emphasis has been laid on understanding and communicating with one's individual self in order to engage effectively and positively with others without much bias. The interactive elements are built on the pillars of "Faith, Practice and Study," which are core to Buddhist practice. In order to build on individual faith there has to be concrete and actual experience. Thus to develop faith, action has to be taken and confidence gained through practice and understanding of what Buddhism really entails. In the practice of Buddhism, much emphasis is placed on the significance of undergoing an inner transformation that will enable individuals to bring out their best human qualities and ability to change their circumstances through a revolution of character.

Ikeda encourages sharing with others – a principle and practice that develops individuals' inner potential, consciously or subconsciously, towards enlightenment. He believes that through continuous interaction, people can grow and become enlightened.

SSN's approaches, as stated previously, lay more emphasis on political engagements. Dialogue through direct contact with conflicting parties essentially remains the most widely used communicative tool in the network's various engagements.

Amongst the commonalities that can be found between the two, both Ikeda and SSN believe in the use of person-to-person encounters and communication, as well as publications as channels of dialogue. The emphasis here is laid on translating the mending of human relations through discussions and published texts. The publications provide a framework that informs and addresses the larger audiences on how we should work together. Similarly, the persons-to-persons discussions/interactions develop the potential to understand underlying problems in-depth and seek balanced solutions to them.

Another common factor in Ikeda's and SSN's work is the cross-cultural approach which both use to engage the different actors caught in conflicts. These can be witnessed in the several international discussions and meetings held by Ikeda himself, and by the institutions he has established, and the various international peace process workshops and field missions co-organized by SSN. These gestures of cross-cultural dialogue have opened doors to a better understanding of the complexities and genesis of most conflicts in Africa, Asia, and Latin America. The principles and practices have helped both Ikeda's and SSN's practitioners to recognize the satisfaction and growth that accompany their efforts to truly help others identify and address the problem, mitigate and restore relations and trust amongst the warring parties while trying to manage the conflicts within their respective countries and communities.

Principles of dialogue

When considering the issue of "sustainable peace," what are we actually saying? I believe the assumption here is that we are mostly concerned with the various interventions we apply to solve problems pertaining to politics, economic and/or social-cultural issues. In this context, dialogue remains a key tool for sustainable peace, growth and development. It is a tool that has been overlooked by many practitioners but has proved to be very significant in breaking deadlocks amongst conflicting parties, whether at inter-community or state levels.

By recognizing that no two human beings can think or act in exactly the same way, principles of dialogue are instrumental in fostering relationships with the key objective of reaching an understanding among the different portions of organizations and restoring broken interpersonal relations. When we learn to communicate through our minds, hearts and souls with the desire to connect to the spirit in self and others in order to act for the higher good of all, we will be on the way to high performance, understanding, peace, harmony and spiritual progress.

In my view, there are two fundamental values that each human being needs to practice for a fruitful dialogue to take place: respect for each person, and trust in the process of dialogue. A unique relationship develops among team members who enter into dialogue regularly. They develop a deep trust that cannot help but carry over into discussions. They develop a richer understanding of the uniqueness of each person's point of view. They experience how larger understandings emerge by holding one's own point of view "gently" (Senge 1990).

Effective dialogue is a skill as well as a gift that not many of us possess, especially in the sense that many of us, during conversations, already have preconceived ideas or perceptions about certain topics or issues. How well do we know ourselves; how do we put aside our views and listen to others'; how do we strike a balance in case our view is different from others' and still remain impartial? As peacebuilders, these are some of the questions we need to ask ourselves as constant reminders during our field mission activities as well as other international fora for discussions.

Here I would like to add that I believe that spiritual inspiration of any type can be beneficial for the practice of effective dialogue. In Buberian terms, the theologian's primary frame of reference is the act of prayer, where the communication positions the "thou," this intimate second person, as God.[4] Dialogue calls for one to practice or possess inner tranquility. Inner tranquility by itself calls for one to practice humility amidst challenges and hardships as can be found in the Quranic verse, "I [Allah The Almighty] will send an illiterate messenger; he will be neither impolite, rough nor noisy in the markets. He will not be obscene or vulgar. I will make him tranquil and good." This verse can be likened to the biblical verses of the beatitudes, specifically "Blessed are the meek, for they shall inherit the earth. Blessed are those who hunger and thirst for righteousness, for they shall be filled. Blessed are the peacemakers for they shall be called sons of God."

Counterparts in seeking global peace

The rigor and creativity shown in unpacking the problems and proposing solutions proves, to me at least, that solutions can be found.[5] Looking at Ikeda's concerns as well as SSN's, I can see good reasons for the two parties to further explore their collaborations since both believe in the principle of dialogue as a step to finding solutions to problems. Ikeda's active participation in attempts to attain global peace, as well as activities of the institutions he represents and SSN's tricontinental human resources, could be a key to a "new partnership" with special attention to Africa, especially the conflict-stricken regions of the Democratic Republic of Congo and Darfur in Sudan. Africa continues to lag behind despite tremendous attempts to adapt to globalization. Through SSN's *Learning Exchange and Research & Information Resource* activities, links can be found with Ikeda's activities and/or the institutions he represents, and it would be worth exploring further Ikeda's concept of "promoting cultural and educational exchange, grassroots exchange" (*SGI Quarterly* 2009b, 25).

Conclusion

The sustainability of peace at all levels (individual, community, society, national or global) may be threatened at any given time and therefore constantly calls for continuous dialogue in order to find appropriate solutions to address the problems and disagreements that are being experienced.

By tapping into our potential, we can find unlimited wisdom, courage, hope, confidence, compassion, vitality and endurance. Instead of avoiding or fearing our problems, we learn to confront them with joyful vigor, confident in our ability to surmount whatever life throws in our path (SGI-USA 1998).

The absolute end result of people interacting and talking "with" each other as opposed to talking "at" each other, is for people to understand one another.

It has never been an easy task for two strongly opposing opinions to strike an equilibrium or balance a scale fairly. The reason for this is that no one opinion is ready to succumb to the other, probably because of fear of the unknown, but also because of fear of the known. This fear could take the form of fear of losing authority or recognition; fear of facing the consequences of prior actions or decisions made; fear of being seen as weak or vulnerable; fear of being seen to have limited negotiating power; and many other reasons that the conscious mind may perceive or be unaware of.

However, through recurrent and tireless engagements in talks and discussions, whether at the individual, community, domestic or international levels, barriers eventually ease and the paths to comprehending motives and actions concurrently open. It is through endless dialoguing that solutions are sought and eventually peace is achieved. Several elements, such as mediation discussions and conferences and field research missions, may play an active role in this process. The end result would always be achieving peace amongst parties in mild or severe disagreements.

Scholars, theologians, philosophers, academicians, and researchers may all have different definitions of the concepts of dialogue and peace. As peacebuilders, it is important to constantly step back from our absorbing duties and take a moment to ask our individual self, "Am I at peace with myself and with those around me?" This may seem like a very limited philosophy or theory, but it is actually quite practical and effective for those who are genuinely in search of a concrete solution to an over-extended problem. Unfortunately, it is rarely practiced by us, the so-called "peacebuilders," whether domestically or internationally. The main reason could be that as individuals we rarely take time for self-reflection and inner transformation in this world troubled with constant global squabbles, economic struggles, social injustices, and many other societal mishaps. This means that our inner selves are constantly at war, rarely allocating time for dialogue. And yet we expect to achieve "Global Peace" with others. This is a problem that should raise concern in genuine peacebuilders; those dealing with armed groups, legitimate states at conflict, unrest in communities/societies and other sources of potential direct violence.

During peace negotiations we have seen that the principle of using the dialogue mechanism is vital, establishing the strong link between the quality and effectiveness of the dialogue/negotiations and the final product, peace agreements and – ideally – a much improved long-term relationship between the parties. We find in specific contexts of the four most practiced religions in the world – Islam, Christianity, Hinduism, and Buddhism – verses and texts relating to the search for inner peace by humans as a way to achieve reconciliation with the self and others. Here I am not suggesting that a lot of emphasis be placed on religion when seeking a solution to a conflict situation, but rather on the religious factors that stress constant self-reflection and discovery when humanity finds itself between a "rock and a hard place." It is important for this element to be factored in by mediators during peace negotiations and reflected in the final agreements. It can be used as a strategy to soften stubborn persistence during talks and at the same time to ensure perseverance and continuity of the negotiations by the warring parties and the mediators.

Earlier, some highlights of the various concepts regarding a philosophy of peace within the context of Islam, Hinduism, Christianity, and Buddhism were also discussed. It would be interesting and important for scholars and peacebuilders to discuss in greater detail how those practicing the mentioned faiths undergo inner transformation that enables individuals to bring out the best human qualities and abilities through a revolution of character. The findings of these exchanges could thereafter be used as templates and be applied as cross-border strategies by international peacebuilders seeking solutions to some of the conflicts being witnessed in Africa, Asia, Latin America, and some parts of the Middle East. Understanding the inner transformation perspectives and processes inspired by various religious practices could be used as a new guiding tool for international peace negotiations and settlements.

If all *genuine peacebuilders* were to go back to the drawing board of self-reflection before administering remedies to conflicts we could be assured of attaining global peace in the shortest time possible. It is very important that as peacebuilders our mind understands its own activity, as well as the intertwined effects on dialogue that our religious conditioning and social upbringing have, among other factors. Both SSN and organizations supported by Ikeda could jointly initiate mechanisms or modify the existing ones and forge new approaches to international peacebuilding strategies.

Appendix 1: List of abbreviations and acronyms

AICHR	ASEAN Intergovernmental Commission on Human Rights
ASEAN	Association of Southeast Asian Nations
CPA	Comprehensive Peace Agreement
DDPD	Doha Document for Peace in Darfur
DDR	Disarmament, Demobilization and Reintegration
ECOWAS	Economic Community of West African States
GAM	Free Aceh Movement
GoS	Government of Sudan
GoSL	Government of the Republic of Sierra Leone
GRP	Government of the Republic of the Philippines
HR	human rights
IHL	International Humanitarian Law
LoGA	Law on Governing Aceh
MILF	Moro Islamic Liberation Front
MNLF	Moro National Liberation Front
MoU	Memorandum of Understanding
NSAGs	non-state armed groups
RUF	Revolutionary United Front
SALW	small and light weapons
SPLM/A	Sudan People's Liberation Movement/Army
SSG/R	Security Sector Governance/Reform
SSN	South–South Network
UNAMSIL	United Nations Mission in Sierra Leone

Appendix 2: SSN's Programs, Networks/Partners and Achievements

a) Learning Exchange **Programme,** (Co-)Organized international forums:

- in November 2005, co-sponsorship with the Third World Studies Center (TWSC), University of the Philippines (UP) of a roundtable discussion in Manila with co-editor Eric G. Berman on the Small Arms Survey-Geneva 2005 book *Armed and Aimless: Armed Groups, Guns and Human Security in the ECOWAS {West Africa} Region*
- in November 2005, SPRC (Sudan) – NURC (Rwanda) one week

Exchange Visit, themed *'Sharing Experiences and Lessons Learnt'*, held in Rwanda

- in November 2006, sponsorship of Philippine launching-forums in Manila and Mindanao on the International Council on Human Rights Policy (ICHRP)-Geneva 2006 report *Negotiating Justice? Human Rights and Peace Agreements*, with the Mindanao forum co-sponsored with the Technical Assistance Center for the Development of Rural and Urban Poor (TACDRUP)-Davao City
- in March 2008, co-sponsorship with the Hiroshima University Partnership for Peacebuilding and Social Capacity (HiPeC) of the Experimental Peace Research Workshop on "Ceasefire and Development: To Share the Experiences towards Peace" in Hiroshima, with the participation of representatives of the Governments of Sudan and the Philippines, the Sudan People's Liberation Movement/Army (SPLM/A) and the Moro Islamic Liberation Front (MILF)
- in May 2009, through the Committee on Accountability of Non-State Armed Groups (CALASAG) which SSN co-convened, co-sponsorship with *Paghiliusa sa Paghidaet-Negros* (PsP-N, Solidarity in Peace) and Human Rights Defenders (HRD) in Negros of a roundtable discussion in Bacolod City on human rights violations and accountability of NSAGs.

b) Direct Engagement Programme, SSN and its affiliates has been involved with:

- participation in regional field missions with SPLM/A in the current Sudan Peace Process post-2005 settlement
- special discussion meeting with MILF representatives who attended a November 2006 SSN forum in Mindanao on the ICHRP 2006 report *Negotiating Justice? Human Rights and Peace Agreements*
- discussion interactions on peace frameworks with representatives of four Philippine rebel groups – MILF, Moro National Liberation Front (MNLF), *Rebolusyonaryong Partido ng Manggagawa ng Mindanao* (RPM-M, Revolutionary Workers Party of Mindanao), and Cordillera People's Liberation Army (CPLA) – during the above-mentioned November 2006 workshop in Mindanao on "The Engagement of Armed Groups in Peace Processes"

- continuing NSAG engagement work of several SSN-Asia affiliates and partners on various fronts and issues, for example: Nonviolence International (NI) Southeast Asia-Bangkok with certain Burmese ethnic armed groups; and Sulong CARHRIHL with the Communist Party of the Philippines (CPP)-New People's Army (NPA)-National Democratic Front of the Philippines (NDFP) in various local levels.

c) Research and Information Resource **Programme, SSN and its affiliates has:**

- printed publications: Report on the SPRC (Sudan) – NURC (Rwanda) Exchange Visit of November 2005
- developed Proceedings of the March 2008 Experimental Peace Research Workshop on "Ceasefire and Development: To Share the Experiences towards Peace," co-published with Hiroshima University Partnership for Peacebuilding and Social Capacity (HiPeC)
- comprehensively carried out a field research and published a book, *Primed and Purposeful: Armed Groups and Human Security Efforts in the Philippines*, co-published with Small Arms Survey-Geneva in 2009
- presented SSN-related papers and/or distributed during some of the above-mentioned as well as other regional and international workshops and forums.

d) Mechanism Development **Programme, part of SSN's achievements include:**

- presented a preliminary paper proposing "NSAGs engaged in peace processes" as a new international legal category and incentive for NSAGs to supplement existing IHL categories
- through its affiliate Philippine Campaign to Ban Landmines (PCBL), developed and initiated four signings in 2008 of a new instrument for NSAGs to adhere to, become accountable for, and generate assistance for compliance with the key norms, standards and undertakings of existing IHL on landmines, entitled "Rebel Group Declaration of Adherence to International Humanitarian Law on Landmines."

e) Advocacy & Networking **Programme, SSN has acquired:**

Strategic partners at the international level. SSN has been able to establish good working relations through the afore-mentioned activities and projects with several international/regional NGOs/institutes, including:

a. Small Arms Survey–Geneva

b. International Council on Human Rights Policy (ICHRP)–Geneva

c. The Redress Trust (REDRESS)–London

d. Conciliation Resources (C-R)–London

e. Southeast Asia Coalition to Stop the Use of Child Soldiers (SEACSUCS)–Bangkok/then Manila

f. Hiroshima University Partnership for Peacebuilding and Social Capacity (HiPeC), Japan

g. Centre for the Study of Radicalisation and Contemporary Political Violence (CSRV), Department of International Politics, Aberystwyth University, Wales, UK

h. Toda Institute for Global Peace and Policy Research, Japan/ Hawai'i–USA.

CHAPTER 8

SGI's Dialogical Movement to Achieve a World without Nuclear Weapons

Kimiaki Kawai

Conflict does not make dialogue impossible, it makes it necessary.
– Daisaku Ikeda, President,
Soka Gakkai International (2010a)

Daisaku Ikeda is convinced that the only ultimately viable response to the threat posed by nuclear weapons is to be found in dialogue. He is convinced that communication between and among people has the power to counter and eliminate this existential threat to humankind.

Is this a purely quixotic assertion? At first sight, there is an enormous asymmetry between the power of nuclear weapons – a single one of which can instantaneously destroy an entire city – and people coming together to talk. Yet Ikeda's confidence in the power of dialogue has remained unshaken for decades. If anything, it has deepened with the passing of time. This chapter seeks to explore the rationale underlying Ikeda's efforts to pursue dialogue and exchange as a means of realizing a world free of nuclear weapons. Central to this is the worldview, the perspectives on life, people and society, that inform Buddhism, particularly the Buddhism of Nichiren Daishonin (1222–82)[1] that Ikeda and his fellow Soka Gakkai International (SGI) members active around the world embrace.

The nature of nuclear weapons

Before entering into an analysis of the particular Buddhism-based perspective on nuclear weapons that Ikeda holds, I would like to address some of the salient features of nuclear weapons which are often cited by those who oppose them and seek their abolition. I will do this from the following perspectives: (1) effects on life, (2) military value, (3) incompatibility with "human security," and (4) growing fears of the dangers of terrorism.

Effects on life

Nuclear weapons are known for their devastating, multigenerational impacts on human lives and the natural environment. Nuclear weapons can instantly slaughter vast numbers of people, as was experienced in Hiroshima and Nagasaki. The survivors are condemned to a lifetime of suffering from the aftereffects of radiation – a lasting burden of misery that will be visited on subsequent generations in the form of genetic mutations and illnesses. Further, a full-scale nuclear war would result in a condition which Jonathan Schell (1982, 119) has called "the death of death" – a ravaging of life on Earth so thorough that the contrasting concept of "death" would cease to have meaning.

From the point of view of non-human life, the natural environment, there is the prospect of irreversible damage to the Earth's climate; the so-called "nuclear winter." In this scenario, the detonation of large numbers of nuclear weapons, and the resulting catastrophic fires, would release large amounts of smoke and soot into the stratosphere. The dramatic reduction in sunlight reaching the Earth's surface would produce severe cold and other climatic change. As Tilman Ruff, chair of the International Campaign to Abolish Nuclear Weapons (ICAN) warns, "[r]ecent studies by some of the world's foremost atmospheric scientists have confirmed not only that these effects would be more severe and prolonged than previously thought, but that abrupt global cooling, unprecedented in recorded human history, would follow a regional nuclear war involving 100 Hiroshima-size nuclear weapons" (Ruff 2010, 5).

Military value

Even within the context of war, it must be said that nuclear weapons have only the most "limited" military value. This is intimately linked to the legal principle of proportionality – that force must be wielded in proportion to the military objective it seeks to achieve. In his dissenting opinion in the 1996 International Court of Justice Advisory Opinion on the question of the legality of the threat or use of nuclear weapons, Judge Christopher Weeramantry explained that nuclear weapons "went beyond the purposes of war." Referring to Aristotle's view that "war must be looked upon simply as a means to peace"[2] rather than an end in itself, he argues that "a war which destroys the other party is totally lacking in meaning and utility, and hence totally lacks justification" (Weeramantry 1996, 524).

Nuclear weapons are also widely considered to be incompatible with another bedrock principle of international humanitarian law: that the weapons and means of waging war must distinguish between combatants and noncombatants (soldiers and civilians) and all efforts must be made to avoid harming the latter. The nature of nuclear weapons – the unparalleled scale of their destructive force – makes it virtually impossible that this distinction could be respected. From these perspectives, it is argued that nuclear weapons cross all imaginable boundaries of legitimacy as military weapons.

Incompatibility with human security

A third perspective from which nuclear abolition is argued is that of "human security." That is, there is no justification for sacrificing such imperatives as clean water, safe food and healthcare – all essential to the lives and well-being of ordinary people – in order to continue building and maintaining nuclear weapons. Even if they are never actually used, the development, manufacture and testing of nuclear weapons give rise to serious long-term radiation and health concerns. In this view, nuclear weapons are fundamentally in irreconcilable conflict with the goals of human security; they are a reflection of distorted security priorities.

Growing fears of threats of nuclear terrorism

The last point that should be dealt with is an emerging concern shared by the public and decision-makers alike: the threat of nuclear terrorism. With thousands of nuclear warheads still in existence, our world is faced with the growing dangers of nuclear terrorism. UN Secretary-General Ban Ki-moon has called this "one of the most serious threats of our time" (Ban Ki-moon 2007). To counter this threat it is urgent to prevent proliferation, to further disarmament and to take special measures to ensure that terrorists do not acquire nuclear materials or weapons.

For such "non-state actors" – with nothing to protect and nothing to lose – the logic of nuclear deterrence[3] means nothing. A deep psychological continuity can be observed between the threat of annihilation based on the deterrence theory and the nihilistic eagerness to use nuclear weapons on the part of terrorists; both manifest a willingness to devastate or wipe out people and societies perceived as "other" in order to achieve political objectives.

In view of the effects of nuclear weapons from these perspectives, those who oppose nuclear weapons argue that their continued existence represents a grave threat to humankind's welfare and even existence.

Ikeda opposes war in principle and so, as may be expected, has never entered into a detailed discussion of (2) the military value or efficacy of nuclear weapons. He has, however, repeatedly addressed (1) the devastating impact on human life and (3) the conflict between these weapons and the imperatives of human security. His writings also indicate his awareness of the growing concerns over nuclear terrorism. Ikeda's opposition to nuclear weapons includes these "secular" aspects but is not limited to them. To these reasons, he appends a Buddhist commitment to and faith in the limitless value, dignity and potential of human life which will be introduced later. For him, it is these aspects of human life that make the abolition of nuclear weapons both imperative and possible.

Ikeda's commitment to dialogue

Ikeda's commitment to dialogue is not limited to the question of the abolition of nuclear weapons; he considers it the best means of responding to any form of conflict. While recognizing the difficulties of conducting dialogue, he rejects violence as an alternative: "[t]he fact is that there are cases where it seems that there is no dialogue partner, or that the burdens of the past make dialogue impossible. But, however justified it may appear, resort to violence and force ultimately resolves nothing" (Ikeda 2008a). In contrast, "conflict resolution through dialogue – unlike military force whose essence is destruction – holds the promise of a genuine and lasting solution" (Ikeda 2008a).

How does Ikeda understand dialogue? He describes dialogue, its challenges and possibilities, in this way:

> Dialogue starts from the courageous willingness to know and be known by others. It is the painstaking and persistent effort to remove all obstacles that obscure our common humanity. Genuine dialogue is a ceaseless and profound spiritual exertion that seeks to effect a fundamental human transformation in both ourselves and others (...) [T]he energy generated by this courageous effort can break the chains of resignation and apathy that bind the human heart, unleashing renewed confidence and vision for the future (Ikeda 2007a).

In this way, Ikeda asserts that dialogue can help us take the next step forward to acknowledge our human commonalities, both positive and negative, empowering people to work for a shared future.

Ikeda has been a steadfast practitioner of dialogue. Since becoming third president of Soka Gakkai in 1960, he has consistently engaged in dialogue, meeting with more than 7,000 leading political, cultural and intellectual figures from different cultural, religious, social and political backgrounds.

One period of particular note is the years 1974–75, a time of heightened Cold War tensions, when strains between China and the Soviet Union threatened to erupt in open conflict. During this period, Ikeda traveled repeatedly to China, the Soviet Union and the US in a private capacity, engaging such figures as Chinese Premier Zhou Enlai (1898–1976), Soviet Premier Aleksey Kosygin (1904–80) and US Secretary of State Henry Kissinger in dialogue and conveying messages between them, as described in chapter 2 of this volume. He urged summit meetings among the leaders of the superpowers, in order to reduce tensions and prevent further escalation of the arms race. Ivan Ivanovich Kovalenko (1919–2005),[4] former deputy director of the International Department of the Communist Party of the Soviet Union, who was instrumental in realizing Ikeda's visit to the Soviet Union in 1974, described Ikeda as an "expert of citizen diplomacy" (Kovalenko 1999).

But Ikeda has made it clear that he does not consider dialogue to be something that can only be practiced meaningfully at a high, diplomatic level. Rather, he is convinced that it is a "challenge that can be taken up by anyone – anytime" (Ikeda 2009a). For him, it is a practical tool readily available to anybody, in any walk of life, position or capacity. It is his belief that dialogue can be understood as a collaborative and creative effort by every citizen toward the future that we inevitably share, based on our common humanity.

Heritage of the mentor

As mentioned, Ikeda's opposition to nuclear weapons is based on the Buddhist understanding that he learned from his mentor and second Soka Gakkai president, Josei Toda (1900–58) that all life has infinite potential and inherent dignity and value. Based on his Buddhist faith, Toda coherently upheld the principle of the inviolable right to life of all human beings.

This principle underlies Toda's opposition to nuclear weapons articulated in his 1957 declaration in which he called for their abolition:

> Because we, the citizens of the world, have an inviolable right to live, anyone who jeopardizes that right is a devil incarnate, a fiend, a monster (…) Even if a country should conquer the world through the use of nuclear weapons, the conquerors must be viewed as devils, as evil incarnate (Toda 1957).

Toda's uncompromising, principled stance – expressed in language of a direct and unyielding moral tenor – stood in contrast to the debates that were then taking place at the domestic Japanese and international levels. Internationally, the Eastern and Western blocs were frantically competing with each other in developing atomic and hydrogen bombs and conducting test blasts. The military and foreign policy establishments in both blocs were largely focused on achieving strategic advantages and turning these to their benefit in the arena of international politics. What has come to be known as the "nuclear taboo" was only beginning to take form.[5] Nuclear weapons were widely considered to be part of the legitimate arsenal of the superpowers, to be used if military logic so dictated.

Within Japan, public opinion against nuclear weapons was galvanized by the 1954 tragedy of the *Daigo Fukuryu Maru*, in which a Japanese tuna fishing boat was exposed to nuclear fallout from the US's Castle Bravo thermonuclear device test on Bikini Atoll. The 23 irradiated crew members suffered severe symptoms of acute radiation syndrome, and one of them died, sparking a widespread antinuclear movement in Japan. However, domestic antinuclear efforts came increasingly to align themselves along the divisions of the Cold War, a trend that became particularly pronounced in the 1960s, with some left-wing opposition justifying Soviet nuclear weapons development as essentially defensive in nature. "Although a movement calling for a ban on the testing of atomic or nuclear weapons has arisen around the world," Toda noted, his intention was to go beyond such partisan divisions to "attack the problem at its root" (Toda 1957) in order to "rip out the claws that lie hidden in the very depths of such weapons" (Ibid.).

Ikeda was among those who attended the meeting in September 1957 at which Toda issued his call for the abolition of nuclear weapons. Toda died in April the following year and Ikeda succeeded him as third Soka Gakkai president in 1960. Ikeda has often referred to Toda's declaration as an enduring inspiration for the Soka Gakkai's peace activities, particularly its efforts to abolish nuclear weapons. Writing in 2006, he offered the following interpretation of Toda's philosophy: "Because Toda saw nuclear weapons as an absolute evil, he was able to transcend ideology and national interest (...) Today, half a century later, the language of nuclear deterrence and 'limited' nuclear war is again in currency. I am convinced that Toda's soul-felt cry, rooted in the deepest dimensions of life, now shines with an even brighter universal brilliance" (Ikeda 2006a).

In September 2007, the 50th anniversary of Toda's declaration, Ikeda reflected on Toda's spirit in a message delivered to the Civil Society Peace Forum held in New York to commemorate that occasion. In it, he wrote: "Toda had the insight to understand that the logic that justifies the possession of nuclear weapons grows from the most extreme form of human desire – the desire to dominate and bend others to our will, the readiness to annihilate them, destroying their lives and livelihoods, should they resist" (Ikeda 2007a). He then stated his belief that the life of each individual is an inestimable treasure filled with infinite possibilities, referring to the principal Buddhist teaching that life is the "foremost of all treasures" (Nichiren 1999, 1125). Observing the injunction against killing found in all spiritual traditions, he proclaimed: "No one has the right to rob others of this most precious treasure of life (...) [This] must be the eternal guiding principle for humankind" (Ikeda 2007a). Ikeda thus asserted that, from a Buddhist perspective, nuclear weapons represent "the most extreme form of human desire." They are, in other words, a culmination of extreme self-centeredness, which deny others the right to live.

Two years later, in 2009, Ikeda offered a further interpretation of the underlying message of the 1957 declaration:

> If we are to put the era of nuclear terror behind us, we must struggle against the real "enemy." That enemy is not nuclear weapons per se, nor is it the states that possess or develop them. The real enemy that we must confront is the ways of thinking that justify nuclear weapons; the readiness to annihilate others when they are seen as a threat or as a hindrance to the realization of our objectives (Ikeda 2009b).

This statement summarizes Ikeda's thinking about the psychology underlying the development and deployment of nuclear weapons. He seeks here, as elsewhere, to cast the problem in human – and not simply technical or geopolitical – terms. As he stated in his November 2006 meeting with International Atomic Energy Agency (IAEA) Director Mohamed ElBaradei: "Nuclear weapons are a human invention. Given this fact, it cannot be beyond our capacity to abolish them" (Ikeda 2006b). This statement implies that abolition of nuclear weapons requires more than getting rid of them physically; this is merely one of many aspects of the problem. He pointed out: "Even if all nuclear arsenals are eliminated, the serious question will remain as to how to deal with the knowledge of nuclear arms production that has been acquired by humankind" (Ikeda 1997). The fact is that nuclear weapons-related technology will remain even after the last warhead has been dismantled; they "cannot be uninvented."[6] Unless we change the ways of thinking that justify the readiness to annihilate others, he has asserted, such technology will remain available in potential and can even enable the production of other even more inhumane weapons in the future (Ikeda 1998).

Ikeda attributes the ultimate cause of such destructive ways of thinking to "a loss of awareness of the interrelatedness and inseparability of one's own lives and those of others – human or otherwise" (Ikeda 2010b). When people lose sight of a sense of interrelatedness, they do not see that destroying others means destroying themselves. In the context of security, such thinking is based on the delusion that we can protect our own self-interest and build our own security by terrorizing and sacrificing others. It has a corollary in the "us versus them" attitude that ElBaradei described:

> We continue to emphasize our differences instead of what we have in common. We continue to talk about "us" versus "them." Only when we can start to talk about "us" as including all of humanity will we truly be at peace (Ikeda 2006b).

Ikeda and ElBaradei shared the concern that if we lose sight of the reality of the interdependent nature of life, this inevitably leads us to the kind of egoism that justifies discrimination or even violence against others. Ikeda expressed this idea on another occasion, when he said: "it is impossible to construct one's own happiness and security on the fear and suffering of others" (Ikeda 2007a).

Ikeda has often used the term "human revolution" (Ikeda 2007b) – popularized in the post-World War II period by Toda – to describe the fundamental transformation of consciousness that leads to positive action. At the heart of this transformation is an awakening to the interrelatedness and inseparability of all life. Ikeda characterizes this as a revolution "open to all" (Ikeda 2007b) and "one that does not demand the sacrifice of a single life" (Ikeda 2007b). In the context of the movement toward a nuclear-free world, it is a "revolution" of consciousness, a dramatic change in our perception of "security." Ikeda has further elaborated on how we can make progress in this endeavor through inner transformation: "When this process achieves a critical momentum – with waves of positive change spreading from one person to another – global society itself will be dramatically transformed" (Ikeda 2007b). It is Ikeda's belief that profound transformation within individuals – an awakening to the preciousness of our own lives, the lives of others, and to the indissoluble linkages between our own lives and those of others – can provide the basis for popular solidarity opposing nuclear weapons. Communicated through global civil society, this popular will can ultimately have an irresistible impact on policy-making processes, moving them inexorably toward the elimination of nuclear weapons. He has outlined the core logic of this transformation in the following terms:

> If nuclear weapons epitomize the forces that would divide and destroy the world, they can only be overcome by the solidarity of ordinary citizens, which transforms hope into the energy to create a new era (Ikeda 2009b).

Function of dialogue

SGI's activities toward a nuclear-weapon-free world are based on the conviction that a change in the human heart can spark changes leading to a triumph over the violence that is epitomized by nuclear weapons. This does not mean, however, that we must wait passively until human nature fundamentally improves before nuclear weapons can be eliminated. From Ikeda's Buddhist perspective, working for nuclear abolition is a proactive manifestation of empathetic solidarity with the entire human species and all life on this planet. As such it can catalyze a shift in our views and attitudes toward others, empowering people to resist and overcome the deep-rooted impulse toward self-centeredness. In this sense, he considers that the inner transformation of human revolution is as much a "process" (Ikeda 2007b) as an outcome, a vehicle and a goal.

All religious traditions can serve as a source of hope where there is seemingly no objective justification for it. For SGI members, Buddhist perspectives have been a source of continued inspiration, serving to sustain their efforts and confidence in ultimate victory – whether in the challenges of individual life or such planetary challenges as nuclear abolition. This can be seen in the way that Ikeda has interpreted the term "Buddha" – an enlightened person – as "another name for a person of unceasing struggle" (Ikeda 1996, 125) who "take[s] action to construct happiness for people" (Ikeda 1996, 125), developing the inner resources to engage untiringly and joyfully in this effort.

Dialogue plays a central role in SGI members' efforts to transform

themselves and the world. Dialogue is crucial as a process that restores awareness of the interrelatedness and inseparability of one's own lives and others.
Through dialogue, we can learn the interests and concerns we share with
each other through direct exchange and interaction with another. Ikeda has
often cited the parable of Bodhisattva Never Disparaging (Skt *Sadāparibhūta*),
which appears in the Lotus Sutra (the Mahayana text particularly prized by
Nichiren) as an exemplar of persistent engagement with others and a model
for dialogic efforts (Ikeda 2009c).

Never Disparaging is described as having lived in the remote past. It was
his Buddhist practice to bow in reverence to everyone he met and to praise
the Buddha nature inherently possessed by each individual. This, however,
only provoked violence and abuse in return as those to whom he bowed were
unable to believe either in their own potential or the ability of this lowly
bodhisattva (his appearance was not particularly inspiring) to discern that
potential. Never Disparaging remained undeterred by their negative reactions. He would simply retreat to a safe distance and repeat his obeisance,
honoring the potential for good even within his persecutors. Over time, as a
result of these actions, Never Disparaging was not only able to develop his
own Buddha nature but also to inspire those who had despised him to become
his disciples, recovering trust in themselves and others and thus entering the
path of attaining Buddhahood themselves.[7]

As Ikeda has stated: "Dialogue has the power to inspire inner change in
people and leads to positive action to transform society. This is the approach
found in the wisdom of the Buddhist tradition since the days of Shakyamuni"
(Ikeda 2006c).

Organizational efforts

In the daunting challenge of achieving a nuclear-free world, nothing is more
vital than to help people develop and maintain confidence that the world can
indeed be changed, thus expanding the circles of people who are engaged in
taking action. Since the end of the Cold War era, perceptions of the imminent
threat and personal relevance of nuclear issues have receded. Many people
seem at least to passively accept the idea that nuclear weapons are a necessary
evil. Others seem to feel hopeless and powerless in the face of this vast and

complex problem, which they assume can only be addressed by governments and authorities.

Ikeda has written that: "In order to revive and re-energize efforts for nuclear disarmament, we need to challenge the persistent notion that nuclear weapons are a 'necessary evil'" (Ikeda 2008b). For SGI, the question has been how we can get so-called ordinary people, immersed in the complexities of day-to-day living, to pay attention to an issue that is seemingly abstract and distant, but which actually has paramount relevance to their lives. It is necessary to develop a common strategy among people at the grassroots level in order to create a great demand for a world without weapons, and to express this through civil society to impact policy makers who are responsible in democratic societies for implementing the popular will.

SGI's nuclear abolition efforts aspire to inform people about present realities, encourage reflection and inspire a sense of empowerment. To these ends, SGI has developed a wide range of activities such as exhibitions, petition drives and lectures as well as a set of educational tools such as DVDs and websites. All of these tools and activities have in common the fact that they are designed to provide "fora for dialogue" in a wide range of settings.

Over the decades SGI has organized numerous exhibitions on this theme. "Nuclear Arms: Threat to Our World" was launched in 1982 in support of the UN World Disarmament Campaign. It was updated as "Nuclear Arms: Threat to Humanity" in 1996. As of 2002, these exhibitions had provided more than 1.6 million people in a total of 39 cities in 24 countries with the opportunity to learn about the realities of nuclear weapons by viewing firsthand the impacts of their use. In efforts driven principally by the youth membership, SGI conducted major petition drives calling for the abolition of nuclear weapons in 1974, 1997–98 and 2010. In each case, millions of signatures were presented to the process of the Treaty on the Non-Proliferation of Nuclear Weapons (NPT) and/or the UN headquarters in New York. In addition to conveying a clear expression of popular will for nuclear weapons abolition to national and international leaders, the effort to collect signatures generated a great number of opportunities for youth activists to engage in dialogue with their friends and colleagues.

The People's Decade of Action for Nuclear Abolition (People's Decade) is the latest of SGI's initiatives for a world free of nuclear weapons.[8] In August

2006, in a proposal[9] for reform of the United Nations, Ikeda put forward the idea of a UN decade of action by the world's people for the abolition of nuclear weapons. In line with his idea, SGI launched the People's Decade campaign in September 2007. As noted, this coincided with the 50th anniversary of Toda's antinuclear declaration in 1957.

The stated goal of the People's Decade campaign is to increase the number of people who reject nuclear weapons as an "absolute evil" and to generate an expanding a global grassroots network of individuals and organizations working to achieve a world without nuclear weapons. A particular focus is to build a global citizens network calling for the complete ban of nuclear weapons through a Nuclear Weapons Convention (NWC). To this end, SGI is actively collaborating with the International Campaign to Abolish Nuclear Weapons (ICAN)[10] initiated by International Physicians for the Prevention of Nuclear War (IPPNW),[11] and other antinuclear networks.

As mentioned above, a key approach of the People's Decade campaign is to create fora where people, especially young people, can exchange views, share ideas and experiences to inspire each other. "From a Culture of Violence to a Culture of Peace: Transforming the Human Spirit" (THS) exhibition is a good example of an effort to create fora for learning, exchange and discussion in keeping with Ikeda's philosophy of dialogue. It was officially launched in September 2007 in New York as the kick-off of the People's Decade campaign at the Civil Society Peace Forum. As of January 2011, the exhibition had been translated into English, Spanish, Chinese, Japanese, Thai, Nepali and Italian, and had been shown in schools, libraries, museums and other public and academic venues in over 200 cities in 25 countries and territories around the world including the UN Offices in Geneva and Vienna, parliament houses in New Zealand and Mexico, as well as on university campuses in different countries.

In this exhibition, SGI focuses on the following three goals for raising public awareness of nuclear issues: (1) to clearly articulate and demonstrate what the issues are, (2) to make clear the relevance of nuclear issues to people's daily lives, and (3) to empower people with a clear and easily understandable goal. The exhibition points out that nuclear weapons reign at the peak of a "pyramid of violence" as the most destructive class of weapons in the world today. At the same time, it demonstrates that the pyramid spreads downward and is ultimately grounded into our everyday lives. It addresses the reality that all kinds of conflict such as crime, domestic violence, abuse and even verbal violence are part of a larger "culture of violence." By showing the connections between nuclear weapons and the violence experienced or even overlooked in our everyday lives, it seeks to awaken viewers to the silent violence of apathy in our society. Questioning our "willingness to live comfortably while ignoring the reality that others are in pain,"[12] it invites the viewers to consider, on a personal level, the theme and ultimate question of the exhibition: "is it possible to transform the culture of violence into a culture of peace?"[13]

While the function of such exhibitions in providing fora for dialogue may not be immediately apparent, SGI's exhibitions are, in fact, designed to provide opportunities for visitors to learn the facts, reflect on what they learn, and empower them to take action. In my capacity as an exhibition organizer, I have witnessed many occasions where viewers at one of our exhibition panels spontaneously struck up a conversation with each other. Some of the viewers whom I have met concurred with the need, expressed in the exhibition, for a "change in the human heart" in order to overcome violence, and said they had come to understand how this is "up to each and every one of us." Such feedback convinces me that the exhibition, in fact, has reached viewers with an effective message and helped to catalyze new awareness and action. In his remarks at the opening of the THS exhibition at the Palais des Nations in Geneva in April 2008, UN High Representative for Disarmament, Sergio Duarte noted that SGI's commitment "has been unfailing, even in the face of difficult obstacles" (Duarte 2008) and "helped to inspire younger generations to understand the importance of progress in disarmament, especially in eliminating nuclear weapons" (Duarte 2008).

As polling data has consistently shown,[14] there are few citizens who proactively seek the continued existence of nuclear weapons; there is, in fact, widespread support for the goal of nuclear abolition, even in the nuclear-weapons states. By bringing together and giving form to the unarticulated aspirations and latent energies of the great majority of the world's people, we can start to build concrete momentum and political will for a world without nuclear weapons. Fully articulated and mobilized, such public opinion would be a force beyond the power of anyone to resist or ignore.

Conclusion

I have discussed in this chapter how Ikeda's firm belief in the power of dialogue is actualized in an extensive range of SGI's initiatives for a world without nuclear weapons. These activities aim to provide fora for dialogue where people can encounter, and learn from, each other and build new bonds of solidarity, in this way "dispelling the dark clouds of suspicion that are the consistent backdrop to war and conflict" (Ikeda 2007c). Anybody can play a role in this noble endeavor. Individual efforts for dialogue can actually make a difference, most importantly by countering the deep-rooted human tendency toward the kind of self-centeredness and willful blindness to interdependence that is most destructively manifested in nuclear weapons.

Finally, I believe that people can be united through a great sense of optimism and hope communicated through dialogue. When people are united, not in fear of others, but by hope for a better future, even the vast and daunting challenges of nuclear abolition can be met and overcome. This can be achieved, in Ikeda's words, through a "revolution that starts here, now – in the heart of every one of us" (Ikeda 2007b).

Notes

Chapter 3

1. See John Dewey, *Experience and Nature*, p. 40.
2. See "Competition for Survival" in *Geography of Human Life*, pp. 285–86.
3. Starting in the 1970s Ikeda's thinking began to develop into what Seager calls "the globalization of Buddhist Humanism" away from the rather rigid, orthodox doctrine of Nichiren Shōshū. These developments have coincided with Ikeda's engagement in dialogical exchanges with intellectuals and leaders from outside the Buddhist tradition. It would be an interesting research project to trace the effects of these dialogues on Ikeda's discourse on both Buddhist and secular topics.
4. For more on *agon* and the interdependence of friendship and rivalry see Dror Posta's unpublished doctoral dissertation: "Anteros: On Rivalry between Friends and Friendship between Rivals."
5. On cultural translation, see Judith Butler's "Restaging the universal: Hegemony and the limits of formalism" (2000).
6. Because the concepts in this theory have been developed over a period of more than two millennia in a number of Asian languages and through multiple translations that, in some cases, share surprisingly little common vocabulary, we find several designations for each concept. The theory of the three perceptions is sometimes referred to as the three truths or the threefold truth. Within that theory, each of the three elements has multiple renditions as well. What Ikeda calls "Provisional Perception" or "*ke*," is sometimes described as "worldly mundane truth," "conventional truth," "temporary existence," or "impermanence." What

Ikeda feels more comfortable describing simply as "*kū*" (he is not entirely satisfied with any of the available translations), is sometimes rendered as "supreme truth," "truth of supreme meaning," "emptiness," "Void," "non-substantiality," or "nothingness." Just as Ikeda prefers to stick to the original Japanese, many authors rely on the original Sanskrit version: "Śūnyatā." The concept of the "Middle Way" is sometimes rendered "Middle Path," and Ikeda often uses the Japanese "chū." In working with sources, I try to keep the vocabulary of my commentary consistent with the quoted passages. Once the language of Ikeda is introduced, I try to use the Japanese *ke*, *kū*, and *chū* unless working around cited passages that use different language. In general, I use the different wordings for the same concept interchangeably.

7. Founders of several schools were originally trained Tendai monks, including Hōnen (1122–212), founder of the Pure Land school; Shinran (1173–263), founder of the True Pure Land school; Dōgen (1200–53), founder of the Sōtō Zen school; and Nichiren (1222–82), founder of Nichiren Buddhism, the philosophical tradition from which Ikeda writes.

8. See Nagarjuna's *Fundamental Verses on the Middle Way* (Skt. Mulamadhyamakakarika) Chapter 24, verse eight: "All Buddhas depend on two truths/ In order to preach the Dharma to sentient beings./ The first is the worldly mundane truth./ The second is the truth of supreme meaning."

9. Naturalism, a philosophical tradition that has enjoyed a considerable revival in the last few decades, considers the entirety of existence without remainders to be encompassed within what we call the physical. Some versions of naturalism interpret the physical as that which is accounted for by the natural sciences. Other forms of naturalism regard the physical as encompassing all of experience, even experiences of what has traditionally been considered as not physical, such as the experience of values. When Ikeda describes the domain of *ke* as that of the physical world, he means the physical in the broader sense that encompasses all of experience. I interpret Ikeda's position as naturalistic in this sense.

10. Jim Garrison helped me to see this connection.

11. Ikeda explicitly makes the point of differentiating *chū* from the Confucian

ethical middle way: "the term *middle way* (...) is [sometimes] considered to be even vaguer than *kū*, and superficial students occasionally confuse it with the Confucian idea of the ethical middle way" (Ikeda 1982, 61).

12. Now, a critic might complain that it is essential for a theory of cosmopolitanism, and a philosophy of dialogue within it, to determine the relationship between the universal and the particular, between the absolute and the relative, and that by stating the matter in terms of "mutual inclusiveness" without further definition, Ikeda simply ducks the question. But in fact he does not. The answer Ikeda provides to this question is consistent with the Buddhist principle of "the unification of the three truths:" that in demanding full determination of the relationship between universal and particular, we fall in the trap of the conceptual thinking of "conventional truth," whose function is to classify, define, and organize. Such type of knowledge has its function and proper domain, but the question at hand lies beyond the domain of the conceptual. For Ikeda, the question of the relationship of the universal and the particular belongs to the domain of action. In other words, the relationship cannot be settled a priori, theoretically by means of principles, but it must be approached anew at every encounter with the world, by means of engagement. That is why values not only can, but *need* be created in dialogue.

13. For an account on valuing from a cosmopolitan perspective see Hansen, D.T., Burdick-Shepherd, S., Cammanaro, C., and Obelleiro, G. (2009). "Education, values, and valuing in cosmopolitan perspective," *Curriculum Inquiry* 39, 587–612.

14. In *Daisaku Ikeda's Philosophy of Peace* (2010), Urbain is careful to make clear that for Ikeda a Buddhist interpretation of the nature of reality (ontology) is not an exclusive path to inner transformation. An ontology provides a language to describe the most basic and general aspects of reality. One such language, Buddhist or otherwise, cannot be the exclusively fit account of the moral life. One can attain the expansive life condition of the greater self never having thought of the world in terms of impermanence, potentiality, and dynamic harmony. But if the ontology of the three perceptions provides an accurate picture of the nature of reality, as Ikeda certainly believes, one would fail to attain

the life condition of the greater self if one's conduct *embodies* ignorance of the nature of reality. It is not essential that I employ the language of impermanence to describe the world and to chart a moral path to navigate it, but it is essential that in my moral life I *embody* an understanding of this principle, because attachment to the illusion of permanence is a direct obstacle to enlightenment. Basically Ikeda's position is a kind of limited moral pluralism: there are many valid moral paths to enlightenment, but just not *any* path would do.

15. Four of Ikeda's older brothers were sent to the frontline during World War II and his oldest brother lost his life in battle. See Ikeda, 2007 Peace Proposal, p. 13.

Chapter 5

1. Although it is beyond the scope of this article, Bakhtin's discussion of Goethe's *Bildungsroman*, in particular, draws further parallels with Ikeda, who also writes extensively on the Goethe corpus as a model of humanistic becoming (e.g., Ikeda [2003] 2006). On December 12, 2009, the Weimar Goethe Institute of Germany presented Daisaku Ikeda with a special commendation for his commitment to peace and for his deep understanding and promotion of Johann Wolfgang von Goethe's spiritual legacy.

2. English translations of Ikeda's dialogues published in Japanese are the author's own and should not be considered official.

Chapter 6

1. For a complete list of published dialogues, see O. Urbain, *Daisaku Ikeda's Philosophy of Peace: Dialogue, Transformation and Global Citizenship* (London: I.B.Tauris, 2010), Appendix 4.

2. D. Ikeda, *Humanising Religion, Creating Peace* 2008 Peace Proposal, pp. 17–18. Cf. D. Ikeda and H.G. Cox, *The Persistence of Religion: Comparative Perspectives on Modern Spirituality* (London: I.B.Tauris, 2009).

3. See R.T. McCutcheon, *Manufacturing Religion: The Discourse on Sui Generis*

Religion and the Politics of Nostalgia (Oxford: Oxford University Press, 1997), T. Asad, *Genealogies of Religion: Disciplines and Reasons of Power in Christianity and Islam* (London: Johns Hopkins University Press, 1993) and B.K. Pennington, *Was Hinduism Invented? Britons, Indians and the Colonial Construction of Religion* (Oxford: Oxford University Press, 2005).

4. For literature on cognitive science and religion, see P. Boyer, *The Naturalness of Religious Ideas: A Cognitive Theory of Religion* (Berkeley: University of California, 1994), P. Boyer, *Religion Explained: The Evolutionary Origins of Religious Thought* (New York: Basic Books, 2001), R.N. McCauley and E. Lawson, *Bringing Ritual to Mind: Psychological Foundations of Cultural Forms* (Cambridge: Cambridge University Press, 2002), H. Whitehouse, *Arguments and Icons: The Cognitive, Social, and Historical Implications of Divergent Modes of Religiosity* (Oxford: Oxford University Press, 2000), J. Andresen (ed.), *Religion in Mind: Cognitive Perspectives on Religious Belief, Ritual and Experience* (Cambridge: Cambridge University Press, 2000), S. Atran, *In Gods We Trust: The Evolutionary Landscape of Religion* (Oxford: Oxford University Press, 2002), B.E. Malley, "The Emerging Cognitive Psychology of Religion: A Review Article," *Method and Theory in the Study of Religion*, 8 (1996), pp. 109–141, I. Pyysiäinen, *How Religion Works: Towards a New Cognitive Science of Religion* (Leiden: Brill, 2001), I. Pyysiäinen and V. Antonnen (eds), *Current Approaches in the Cognitive Science of Religion* (London: Continuum, 2002), J. Barrett, "Exploring the Natural Foundations of Religion," *Trends in Cognitive Sciences*, 4 (2000), pp. 29–34.

Chapter 7

1. By inner transformation we mean efforts at self-improvement, through self-scrutiny, reflection, prayer, meditation and other means to look within and make changes.
2. See for instance the comments of Riefqi Muna on SSG (Muna 2010).
3. Soka Gakkai means "Society for the Creation of Value."
4. See Arnaud Laygues: "Translation and the Philosophy of Dialogue." "Buberian" refers to Martin Buber (1878–1965).
5. See David Petrasek (2010).

Chapter 8

1. Nichiren Buddhism is a school of Buddhism centered on the Mahayana Buddhist text, the Lotus Sutra, as interpreted by the 13th-century Japanese monk Nichiren (1222–82).

2. Aristotle: *Politics*, as quoted in Christopher Weeramantry, Dissenting Opinion on "Legality of the Threat or Use of Nuclear Weapons" – International Court of Justice Advisory Opinion of 8 July 1996 (General List No. 95, 1995–98).

3. Deterrence is a military strategy developed during the Cold War by which governments threaten an immense retaliation if attacked, such that potential aggressors are deterred if they do not wish to suffer great damage as a result of an aggressive action. It is especially relevant with regard to the use of nuclear weapons.

4. Kovalenko played a key role in realizing Ikeda's visit to the Soviet Union in 1974 and also attended Ikeda's meeting with Kosygin (*Seikyo Shimbun*, Sept. 8, 1994).

5. See: Nina Tannenwald: *The Nuclear Taboo: The United States and the Non-use of Nuclear Weapons since 1945* (Cambridge: Cambridge University Press, 2007) for a full discussion of normative restraints against the use of nuclear weapons.

6. The Weapons of Mass Destruction Commission, June 2006: "Weapons of Terror: Freeing the World of Nuclear, Biological and Chemical Arms."

7. See "Bodhisattva Never Disparaging" (*SGI Quarterly*, April 2005).

8. For further details, see <http://www.peoplesdecade.org>. Retrieved on July 24, 2012.

9. Ikeda has been publishing his annual peace proposals since 1983 in the hope that they will help deepen the international debate on critically important issues and aid the search for a way out of our present quandary. He has also issued proposals on specific issues, such as UN reform, sustainable development and educational reform.

10. Launched in 2007, ICAN has developed strategies and strengthened networking between national and international campaigners, broadening the abolition movement and building understanding of why a Nuclear Weapons Convention is the most realistic path to zero <http://www.icanw.org>. Retrieved on July 24, 2012.

11. Founded in 1980 and recipient of the 1985 Nobel Peace Prize, IPPNW is a non-partisan federation of national medical organizations in 63 countries, representing thousands of doctors, medical students, health workers, and concerned citizens who are united behind the goal of creating a more peaceful and secure world freed from the threat of nuclear annihilation <http://www.ippnw.org>. Retrieved on July 24, 2012.

12. From the texts of the antinuclear Exhibition: "From a Culture of Violence to a Culture of Peace: Transforming the Human Spirit."

13. From the texts of the antinuclear Exhibition: "From a Culture of Violence to a Culture of Peace: Transforming the Human Spirit."

14. ICAN: Polls: "A Nuclear-Free Majority" <http://www.icanw.org/polls# recent%20polls>. Retrieved on July 24, 2012.

Bibliography

Preface

Ikeda, Daisaku. 1997. *Songs from My Heart, poems and photographs by Daisaku Ikeda,* New York: Weatherhill.

Ikeda, Daisaku. 2004a. *The Human Revolution.* Santa Monica: World Tribune Press.

Ikeda, Daisaku. 2004b. *Fighting for Peace, poems by Daisaku Ikeda.* Berkeley, California: Creative Arts Book Co.

Ikeda, Daisaku. [2007] 2008. "Moving beyond the Use of Military Force." Editorial in the *Japan Times* of 11 January 2007. In *Embracing the Future.* Tokyo: The Japan Times.

Rees, Stuart. 1991. *Achieving Power, Policy and Practice in Social Welfare.* Sydney: Allen & Unwin.

Urbain, Olivier. 2010. *Daisaku Ikeda's Philosophy of Peace: Dialogue, Transformation and Global Citizenship.* London: I.B.Tauris.

Message to the Conference

Toynbee, Arnold. [1966] 1992. *Change and Habit: The Challenge of Our Time.* Oxford: Oneworld.

Weil, Simone. 2001. *The Need for Roots: Prelude to a Declaration of Duties Towards Mankind.* London: Routledge.

Zweig, Stefan. 1964. *The World of Yesterday: An Autobiography.* Lincoln: University of Nebraska Press.

Introduction

Ikeda, Daisaku. 2005. 2005 Peace Proposal: *Toward a New Era of Dialogue: Humanism Explored.* Retrieved from <http://www.daisakuikeda.org/assets/files/pp2005.pdf> on December 3, 2012.

— 2009. 2009 Peace Proposal: *Toward Humanitarian Competition: A New Current in History.* Retrieved from <http://www.daisakuikeda.org/assets/files/pp2009.pdf> on December 3, 2012.

— 2012. "Buddhism Day by Day: Wisdom for Modern Life by Daisaku Ikeda." Wednesday, September 21, 2012. Retrieved from <http://www.sgiusa.com/encouragement/dbd.php?m=9&d=21&y=2012> on December 3, 2012

Urbain, Olivier. 2010. *Daisaku Ikeda's Philosophy of Peace: Dialogue, Transformation and Global Citizenship.* London: I.B.Tauris.

Chapter 1

Ikeda, Daisaku. 1993. "Mahayana Buddhism and Twenty-First Century Civilization." Speech delivered at Harvard University, September 24, 1993.

— 2001. *From the Ashes: A Spiritual Response to the Attack on America.* Emmaus: Rodale Inc. and Beliefnet, Inc.

Makiguchi, Tsunesaburo. 2002. *A Geography of Human Life*, ed. by Dayle Bethel. San Francisco: Caddo Gap Press.

The Lotus Sutra. 1993. Trans. by Burton Watson. New York: Colombia University Press.

Toda, Josei. 1981. *Toda Josei Zenshu* (Collected Works of Josei Toda), vol. 3. Tokyo: Seikyo Shimbunsha. Translated from the Japanese.

Chapter 2

Ikeda, Daisaku. 2008. *The New Human Revolution*, volume 16, chapter "Dialogue."

Ikeda, Daisaku and Arnold J. Toynbee. 1974. *The Toynbee–Ikeda Dialogue – Man Himself Must Choose.* Tokyo, New York & San Francisco: Kodansha International Ltd. (Published in 1976 with another title, see below.)

— 1976. *Choose Life: A Dialogue.* Oxford: Oxford University Press.

Kelly, Ann. 2002. "The Toynbee–Ikeda Dialogue," in *Art of Living: A Buddhist Magazine* (May).

Kuwabara, Takeo. 1976. Translated from Japanese, foreword to *Ningen kakumei to ningen no joken* (Changes Within: The Human Revolution vs. the Human Condition) by André Malraux and Daisaku Ikeda. Tokyo: Ushio Publishing Company.

Seager, Richard. 2006. *Encountering the Dharma: Daisaku Ikeda, Soka Gakkai, and the Globalization of Buddhist Humanism.* Berkeley, California: University of California Press.

Soka University Website <http://www.soka.ac.jp/en/worldwide/beijing.html> retrieved on March 5, 2012.

Toynbee, Arnold. 1934–61. *A Study of History.* Oxford: Oxford University Press.

Chapter 3

Appiah, Kwame Anthony. 2008. "Education for Global Citizenship." *Yearbook of the National Society for the Study of Education*, 107 (1), 83–99.

Beck, Ulrich. 2006. *Cosmopolitan Vision.* Cambridge: Polity Press.

Beck, Ulrich, and Natan Sznaider. 2006. "Unpacking cosmopolitanism for the social sciences: a research agenda." *The British Journal of Sociology*, 57 (1), 1–23.

Benhabib, Seyla. 2006. *Another Cosmopolitanism.* Oxford: Oxford University Press.

Bosco, Ronald, Joel Myerson and Daisaku Ikeda. 2009. *Creating Waldens: an East–West Conversation on the American Renaissance.* Cambridge, MA: Dialogue Path Press.

Butler, Judith. 2000. "Restaging the universal: Hegemony and the limits of formalism." In Judith Butler, Ernesto Laclau, and Slavoj Zizek (eds), *Contingency, hegemony, universality.* London: Verso.

Delanty, Gerard. 2006. The cosmopolitan imagination: critical cosmopolitanism and social theory. *The British Journal of Sociology*, 57 (1), 25–47.

Dewey, John. 1981. *The Later Works of John Dewey, Volume 1, 1925–1953: 1925, Experience and Nature (Collected Works of John Dewey 1882-1953).*

Díez-Hochleitner, Ricardo and Daisaku Ikeda. 2008. *A Dialogue Between East and West: Looking to a Human Revolution.* London: I.B.Tauris.

Gregoriou, Zelia. 2003. "Resisting the pedagogical domestication of cosmo-politanism: From Nussbaum's concentric circles of humanity to Derrida's aporetic ethics of hospitality." *Philosophy of Education*, 3 (3), 257–66.

Gorbachev, Mikhail Sergeyevich, and Daisaku Ikeda. 2005. *Moral Lessons of the Twentieth Century: Gorbachev and Ikeda on Buddhism and Communism.* London: I.B.Tauris.

Goulah, Jason. 2012. "Daisaku Ikeda and Value-Creative Dialogue: A new current in interculturalism and educational philosophy." *Educational Philosophy and Theory*, 44 (9), 997–1009.

Hansen, David. 2008a. "Education viewed through a cosmopolitan prism." *Philosophy of Education*, 206–14.

— 2008b. "Curriculum and the idea of a cosmopolitan inheritance." *Journal of Curriculum Studies*, 40, 289–312.

— 2010a. "Chasing butterflies without a net: Interpreting Cosmopolitanism." *Studies in Philosophy and Education*, 29 (2), 151–66.

— 2010b. "Cosmopolitanism and Education: A view from the ground." *Teachers College Record*, 112 (1), 1-30.

— 2011. *The Teacher and the World: A Study of Cosmopolitanism as Education.* London: Routledge.

Ikeda, Daisaku. 1982. *Life: An Enigma, a Precious Jewel.* Tokyo: Kodansha International.

— 1986. *The Flower of Chinese Buddhism.* New York: Weatherhill.

— 1996. *A New Humanism: The University Addresses of Daisaku Ikeda.* New York: Weatherhill.

— 2002. *The World is Yours to Change (Kimi ga Sekai wo Kaete Iku).* Tokyo: Asahi Shuppansha.

— 2006. *To the Youthful Pioneers of Soka: Lectures, Essays and Poems on Value-Creating Education.* Hachioji, Tokyo, Soka University Student Union.

— 2007. 2007 Peace Proposal: *Restoring the Human Connection: The First Step to Global Peace.* Retrieved from <http://www.daisakuikeda.org/assets/files/pp2007.pdf> on July 25, 2012.

— 2010. *Soka Education: For the Happiness of the Individual.* Santa Monica: Middleway Press.

— 2011. Toward a World of Dignity for All: The Triumph of the Creative Life. Retrieved June 10, 2011, from: http://www.daisakuikeda.org/assets/files/peace2011.pdf.

Makiguchi, Tsunesaburo and Dayle Bethel. 2002. *A Geography of Human Life*. San Francisco: Caddo Gap Press.

Miller, G.D. 2002. *Peace, Value, and Wisdom: The Educational Philosophy of Daisaku Ikeda*. Amsterdam: Rodopi.

Mouffe, Chantal. 2005. *On the Political*. London: Routledge.

Noddings, Nel. 2005. "Global Citizenship: Promises and Problems." In Nel Noddings (ed.), *Educating Citizens for Global Awareness* (pp. 1–21). New York: Teachers College Press.

Nussbaum, Martha. 1996. "Patriotism and Cosmopolitanism." In Martha Nussbaum and Joshua Cohen (eds), *For Love of Country?* Boston: Beacon Press.

Peccei, Aurelio and Daisaku Ikeda. 1984. *Before it is Too Late*. New York: Kodansha America.

Pieterse, Jan Nederveen. 2006. "Emancipatory Cosmopolitanism: Towards an Agenda." *Development and Change*, 37 (6), 1247–257.

Posta, Dror. 2011. "Anteros: On Rivalry between Friends and Friendship between Rivals." Unpublished doctoral dissertation, Teachers College, Columbia University.

Rotblat, Joseph, and Daisaku Ikeda. 2007. *A Quest for Global Peace: Rotblat and Ikeda on War, Ethics, and the Nuclear Threat*. London: I.B.Tauris.

Seager, Richard. 2006. *Encountering the Dharma: Daisaku Ikeda, Soka Gakkai, and the Globalization of Buddhist Humanism*. Berkeley: University of California Press.

Strand, Torill. 2010a. "Introduction: Cosmopolitanism in the Making." *Studies in Philosophy and Education*, 29 (2), 103–9.

— 2010b. The Making of a New Cosmopolitanism. *Studies in Philosophy and Education*, 29 (2), 229–42.

Swanson, Paul. 1989. *Foundations of T'ien T'ai Philosophy: The Flowering of the Two Truth Theory in Chinese Buddhism (Nanzan Studies in Religion and Culture)*. Fremont, CA: Asian Humanities Press.

Tehranian, Majid and Daisaku Ikeda. 2011. *Global Civilization: A Buddhist–Islamic Dialogue*. London: I.B.Tauris.

Todd, Sharon. 2010. "Living in a Dissonant World: Toward an Agonistic Cosmopolitics for Education." *Studies in Philosophy and Education*, 29 (2), 213–28.

Toynbee, Arnold and Daisaku Ikeda. 2008. *Choose Life: A Dialogue*. London: I.B.Tauris.

Tu, Weiming, and Daisaku Ikeda. 2011. *New Horizons in Eastern Humanism: Buddhism, Confucianism and the Quest for Global Peace*. London: I.B.Tauris.

Urbain, Olivier. 2010. *Daisaku Ikeda's Philosophy of Peace: Dialogue, Transformation and Global Citizenship*. London: I.B.Tauris.

Wider, Sarah, and Masao Yokota. 2010. Interview with Professor Sarah Wider. Retrieved June 10, 2011 from <http://www.daisakuikeda.org/sub/resources/commentary/comment-sarah-wider.html>.

Yalman, Nur, and Daisaku Ikeda. 2008. *A Passage to Peace: Global Solutions from East and West*. London: I.B.Tauris.

Chapter 4

Beck, Ulrich. 1992. *Risk Society: towards a new modernity* (Translated by Mark Ritter), London: Sage Publications.

Bohm, David, ed. 2004. *On Dialogue*, Oxon, New York: Routledge Classics.

Giroux, Henri. 1994. "Doing Cultural Studies: Youth and the Challenge of Pedagogy." *Harvard Educational Review*, 64 (3), 278–308.

— 2003. *The Abandoned Generation: Democracy Beyond the Culture of Fear*, New York: Palgrave Macmillan.

Ikeda, Daisaku. [1993] 1995–2013. *The New Human Revolution*, vols 1–24 (ongoing). Santa Monica: World Tribune Press.

— 2000. Peace Proposal, "Peace through Dialogue: A Time to Talk."

— 2002. Peace Proposal, "The Humanism of the Middle Way: Dawn of a Global Civilization.

— 2004. Peace Proposal, "Inner Transformation: Creating a Groundswell for Peace."

— 2005. Peace Proposal, "Toward a New Era of Dialogue: Humanism Explored." Retrieved on August 1, 2012 from <http://www.daisakuikeda.org/assets/files/pp2005.pdf>.

Ikeda, Daisaku and Majid Tehranian. 2003. *Global Civilization: A Buddhist – Islamic Dialogue*. London, New York: British Academic Press.

Johns, Greg. 2007. "Being Creative About Your Blues," *SGI Quarterly*, October.

Lehmann, Martin. 2005. "Cronulla Riots: Left-wing, politically correct journalists slag off Aussie patriotism." *The Australian*, December 13, 2005. <http://www.australian-news.com.au/Cronulla_riots.htm>.

Nettle, Stuart. 2010. "The Cronulla Riots Five Years On", crikey.com. <au/2010/12/10/the-cronulla-riots-five-years-on>.

Strand, Clark. 2008, "Faith in Revolution", Interview with Daisaku Ikeda, *Tricycle*, Winter. Retrieved on August 1, 2012 from <http://www.tricycle.com/interview/faith-revolution>.

Urbain, Olivier. 2010, *Daisaku Ikeda's Philosophy of Peace: Dialogue, Transformation and Global Citizenship*. London, New York: I.B.Tauris.

Chapter 5

Bakhtin, Mikhail M. 1981. "Discourse in the Novel." In M. Holquist (ed.) *The Dialogic Imagination: Four Essays by M. M. Bakhtin*, pp. 259–422. Austin, TX: University of Texas Press.

— 1986. "The *Bildungsroman* and its Significance in the History of Realism (Toward a Historical Typology of the Novel)." In C. Emerson and M. Holquist (eds) *Speech Genres and Other Late Essays*, pp. 10–59. Austin, TX: University of Texas Press.

Derbolav, Josef and Daisaku Ikeda. 1992. *Search for a New Humanity*. New York: Weatherhill.

Freibert, Jo Ann. 2010. "The Challenge of Bullying in U.S. Schools: Resistance and Reaction." In D.M. Moss and T.A. Osborn (eds) *Critical Essays on Resistance in Education*, pp. 159–77. New York: Peter Lang.

Goulah, Jason. 2012. "Daisaku Ikeda and Value-Creative Dialogue: A New Current in Interculturalism." *Educational Philosophy and Theory*, 44(9).

Henningsen, Hans and Daisaku Ikeda. 2009. *Asu wo Tsukuru "Kyoiku no Seigyo": Denmaku to Nihon, Yujo no Katarai* [Shaping the Future: The Sacred Task of Education, A Friendly Conversation – Denmark and Japan]. Tokyo: Ushio.

Hickman, Larry, Jim Garrison and Daisaku Ikeda. 2009. "Ningen Kyoiku e no Atarashiki Choryu: Dyui to Soka Kyoiku, Dai 1 Kai: 21 Seiki ni Hikaru Dyui no Hito to Tetsugaku" [Toward a New Current in Human Education: Dewey and Soka Education, Installment One – The Person and Philosophy of Dewey Shining in the 21st Century]. *Todai* [Lighthouse], 12: 52–67.

— 2010a. "Ningen Kyoiku e no Atarashiki Choryu: Dyui to Soka Kyoiku,

Dai 7 Kai: 21 Seiki ni Hikaru Dyui no Hito to Tetsugaku" [Toward a New Current in Human Education: Dewey and Soka Education, Installment Seven – The State of Education and the Problem of Bullying]. *Todai* [Lighthouse], 6: 52–67.

— 2010b. "Ningen Kyoiku e no Atarashiki Choryu: Dyui to Soka Kyoiku, Dai 9 Kai: 21 Seiki ni Hikaru Dyui no Hito to Tetsugaku" [Toward a New Current in Human Education: Dewey and Soka Education, Installment Nine – The Mission of Universities to Foster the Intellect of the Next Generation]. *Todai* [Lighthouse], 8: 52–67.

Holquist, Michael. 1986. "Introduction." In *Speech Genres and Other Late Essays*, edited by C. Emerson and M. Holquist, ix–xxiii. Austin, TX: University of Texas Press.

— 2004. *Dialogism: Bakhtin and His World (2nd Edition)*. New York, NY: Routledge.

Ikeda, Daisaku. [1968] 1987. "The Key to Peace." In *A Lasting Peace, Volume Two*, 3-15. New York, NY: Weatherhill.

— [1973] 2006. "Be Creative Individuals." In *To the Youthful Pioneers of Soka: Lectures, Essays & Poems on Value-Creating Education*, 19–33. Tokyo: Soka University Student Union.

— 1978. *Watakushi no Rirekisho* [My Recollections]. Tokyo: Seikyo Bunko.

— 1980. *My Recollections*. Santa Monica, CA: World Tribune Press.

— 1992. *The New Human Revolution, Volume 15*. Santa Monica, CA: World Tribune Press.

— [1993] 1996. "Mahayana Buddhism and Twenty-First-Century Civilization: A Speech Delivered at Harvard University, Cambridge." In *A New Humanism: The University Addresses of Daisaku Ikeda*, 151–63. New York: Weatherhill.

— 1998. *Discussions on Youth, Vols 1–2*. Santa Monica, CA: Soka Gakkai.

— 1999. *Faith into Action*. Santa Monica, CA: World Tribune Press.

— 2000. *The Way of Youth: Buddhist Common Sense for Handling Life's Questions*. Santa Monica, CA: Middleway Press.

— 2001. *Soka Education: A Buddhist Vision for Teachers, Students and Parents*. Santa Monica, CA: Middleway Press.

— 2003. *Kyoiku no Seiki e* [Toward the Century of Education]. Tokyo: Daisan Bunmeisha.

— 2004. *Kibo no Seiki e: Kyoiku no Hikari* [Toward a Century of Hope: The Light of Education]. Tokyo: Hoshoin.

— [2003] 2006. "Goethe the Man." In *To the Youthful Pioneers of Soka: Lectures, Essays & Poems on Value-Creating Education.* Tokyo: Soka University Student Union.

— 2010a. *Discussions on Youth (New Edition).* Santa Monica, CA: World Tribune Press.

— 2010b. "Peace Starts with Dialogue." *World Tribune*, February 5, 4–5.

Ikeda, Daisaku and Jen-Hu Chang. 2010. *Kyoiku to Bunka no Odo* [The Noble Path of Education and Culture]. Tokyo: Daisan Bunmeisha.

Ikeda, Daisaku and Tu Weiming. 2007. *Taiwa no Bunmei: Heiwa no Kibo Tetsugaku wo Kataru* [Civilization of Dialogue: On the Hope-filled Philosophy of Peace]. Tokyo: Daisan Bunmeisha.

Sadovnichy, Victor A. and Daisaku Ikeda. 2004. *Gaku wa Hikari: Bunmei to Kyoiku no Mirai wo Kataru* [Learning is Light: On the Future of Civilization and Education]. Tokyo: Ushio.

Vitanova, Gergana. 2005. "Authoring the Self in a Non-Native Language: A Dialogic Approach to Agency and Subjectivity." In J.K. Hall, G. Vitanova and L. Marchenkova (eds) *Dialogue with Bakhtin on Second and Foreign Language Learning: New Perspectives*, pp. 149–69. Mahwah, NJ: Lawrence Erlbaum Associates.

Chapter 6

Asad, T. 1993. *Genealogies of Religion: Disciplines and Reasons of Power in Christianity and Islam.* London: Johns Hopkins University Press.

Boyer, P. 1994. *The Naturalness of Religious Ideas: A Cognitive Theory of Religion* Berkeley: University of California.

Cupitt, D. 1997. *After God: the Future of Religion.* New York: Basic Books.

Derrida, J. and G. Vattimo. 1998. *Religion.* Cambridge: Polity Press.

Ikeda, Daisaku and Majid Tehranian. 2003. *Global Civilization: A Buddhist–Islamic Dialogue.* London: British Academic Press.

Ikeda, Daisaku and Mikhail Gorbachev. 2005. *Moral Lessons of the Twentieth Century: Gorbachev and Ikeda on Buddhism and Communism.* London: I.B.Tauris.

Ikeda, Daisaku and Harvey G. Cox. 2009a. *The Persistence of Religion: Comparative Perspectives on Modern Spirituality*. London: I.B.Tauris.

Ikeda, Daisaku and Nur Yalman. 2009b. *A Passage to Peace: Global Solutions from East and West*. London: I.B.Tauris.

McCutcheon, R.T. 1997. *Manufacturing Religion: The Discourse on Sui Generis Religion and the Politics of Nostalgia*. Oxford: Oxford University Press.

Rappaport, R.A. 1999. *Ritual and Religion in the Making of Humanity*. Cambridge: Cambridge University Press.

Whicher, Olive. 1971. *Projective Geometry: Creative Polarities in Space and Time*. London: Rudolf Steiner Press.

Wilson, Bryan and Daisaku Ikeda. 1984. *Human Values in a Changing World: A Dialogue on the Social Role of Religion*. London: Macdonald.

Chapter 7

African New Testament. 2004. *The African New Testament and Psalms*. Nairobi: Pauline Publications Africa.

Bashiru-Kargbo. 2012. "The Peace Process in Sierra Leone." A short presentation available online, retrieved on November 11, 2012 from <http://www.unimuenster.de/Politikwissenschaft/Doppeldiplom/docs/SL.pdf>.

Comprehensive Agreement. 2011. Comprehensive Peace Agreement between the Government of the Republic of the Sudan and the Sudan People's Liberation Movement/Sudan People's Liberation Army, Nairobi, Kenya, January 9, 2005. (Art. 1.5.3).

Doha Document. 2011. Doha Document for Peace in Darfur: Preamble, p. 9; Chapter II – power sharing and administrative status of Darfur, Art.20, p. 13, 2011).

Ikeda, Daisaku. 2005. Ikeda, Daisaku. 2005. *Towards a New Era of Dialogue; Humanism Explored* (Peace Proposal 2005).

— 2006. "Emerging from the Nuclear Shadow." *Japan Times* online, retrieved on November 11, 2012 from <http://www.japantimes.co.jp/text/eo20060914a3.html>.

— 2009. "Essay on Rajiv Gandhi: A Life of Selfless Commitment to the People" in *SGI Quarterly*, October 2009.

— 2012a. Words of Wisdom by Buddhist philosopher Daisaku Ikeda: <http://www.ikedaquotes.org/human-relatioships/dialogue.html>.

— 2012b. "Lecture Series: The Teachings for Victory. The Four Virtues and the Four Debts of Gratitude" in *Living Buddhism*, October 2012. Retrieved on November 11, 2012 from <http://sgiusapublications.news paperdirect.com/epaper/viewer.aspx>.

Islamweb. 2012. "Tranquility: A characteristic of the Prophets and the righteous – II" Retrieved on November 11, 2012 from <http://www. islamweb.net/womane/nindex.php?page=readart&id=160711>.

Krishnamurti, Jiddu. 1950. "On War and Peace." Bombay, 5th Public Talk, March 12, 1950. Retrieved on November 11, 2012 from <http://www. wisdomportal.com/Peace/Peace-Krishnamurti.html>.

Laygues, Arnaud. 2007. "Translation and the Philosophy of Dialogue." Report on the Ph.D. thesis by Arnaud Laygues *Pour une ethique du tra-ducteur poeticien*, defended at the University of Helsinki on 11 May 2007. Retrieved on November 11, 2012 from <http://usuaris.tinet.cat/apym/ on-line/translation/2008_pym_on_laygues.pdf>.

Muna, Riefqi. 2010. Southeast Asia (section) in "HiPeC II and Hiroshima University: Peacebuilding and Security Sector Governance in Asia; 1st HiPeC Practitioners Seminar," August 2010, p. 8. Retrieved on November 11, 2012 from <http://home.hiroshima-u.ac.jp/hipec/ja/ products/report/ps1.pdf>.

Petrasek, David. 2000. Foreword to *Primed and Purposeful: Armed Groups and Human Security Efforts in the Philippines.* Edited by Diana Rodriguez. A Joint Publication of the South–South Network for Non-State Armed Group Engagement and the Small Arms Survey.

Rotblat, Joseph, and Daisaku Ikeda. 2006. *A Quest for Global Peace: Rotblat and Ikeda on War, Ethics and the Nuclear Threat.* London: I.B.Tauris.

Sangharakshita. 2001. *Dhammapada: The Way of Truth.* Translated from the Pali by Sangharakshita. Birmingham, UK: Windhorse.

Santos Jr., Soliman M., March 2010. *Constructively Engaging Non-State Armed Groups in Asia: Minding the Gaps, Harnessing Southern Perspectives.* Naga City Philippines: South-South Network (SSN) for Non-State Armed Group Engagement. Retrieved on November 11, 2012 from <http:// www.southsouthnetwork.com/constructivelyengagingnsagsnew.html>.

Senge, Peter. 1990. *The Fifth Discipline, The Art and Practice of the Learning Organization*. New York: Currency Doubleday.

SGI Quarterly. 2009a. "Youthfulness." October 2009, p. 28. Tokyo: Soka Gakkai International.

— 2009b. "China – Restoring an Ancient Bond," October 2009, p. 25. Tokyo: Soka Gakkai International.

SGI-USA. 1998. "The Winning Life: An Introduction to Buddhist Practice."

Special Court. 2002. Introduction to the "Agreement for and Statute of the Special Court for Sierra Leone, 16 January 2002." Retrieved on November 11, 2012 from <http://www.icrc.org/ihl.nsf/INTRO/605?Open Document>.

SSN (South–South Network for Non-State Armed Group Engagement). 2012. "Engagement." Retrieved on November 11, 2012 from <http://www.southsouthnetwork.com/engage.htm>.

Urbain, Olivier. 2010. *Daisaku Ikeda's Philosophy of Peace: Dialogue, Transformation and Global Citizenship*. London: I.B.Tauris.

Chapter 8

Ban Ki-moon. 2007. SG/SM/11040 L/T/4404. United Nations, June 13, 2007.

Duarte, Sergio. 2008. Opening Remarks for an Exhibition: From a Culture of Violence to a Culture of Peace: Transforming the Human Spirit at the Palais des Nations, Geneva (April 30, 2008).

Ikeda, Daisaku. 1996. Lectures on the "Expedient Means" and "Life Span" Chapters of the Lotus Sutra, Vol. 2. Tokyo: Soka Gakkai.

— 1997. *A New Horizon of a Global Civilization*. Tokyo: Soka Gakkai.

— 1998. Message to the opening of the exhibition "Nuclear Arms: Threat to Humanity" held in Asuncion, Paraguay. Seikyo Shimbun, September 15, 1998.

— 2006a."Emerging from the Nuclear Shadow." *The Japan Times*, September 14, 2006.

— 2006b. Dialogue with Mohamed ElBaradei. *Seikyo Shimbun*, December 1, 2006.

— 2006c. *Fulfilling the Mission: Empowering the UN*. <daisakuikeda.org>.

— 2007a. Message to the Civil Society Peace Forum held at The Cooper Union (September 8, 2007, New York).

— 2007b. "A Human Revolution: Transforming our Way of Living" (*The Japan Times*, April 12, 2007).

— 2007c. "The Promise of Dialogue: Moving beyond the use of military force." *The Japan Times*, January 11, 2007.

— 2008a. World Needs a Global Culture of Human Rights (Inter Press Service, March 28, 2008).

— 2008b. "Nuclear Arms Are No Longer 'Necessary Evils'" (Inter Press Service, August 1, 2008).

— 2009a. *Toward Humanitarian Competition: A New Current in History.* <daisakuikeda.org>.

— 2009b. *Building Global Solidarity Toward Nuclear Abolition.* <daisakuikeda.org>.

— 2010a. "Buddhist Leader Pushes for Nuclear Abolition Treaty" (IDN-InDepthNews, June 21, 2010).

— 2010b. "Learning to Be Human" (Inter Press Service, January 2010).

Ikeda, Daisaku and Austregesilo de Athayde. 2009c. *Human Rights in the Twenty-First Century – A Dialogue.* London: I.B.Tauris.

Kovalenko, Ivan Ivanovich. 1999. Congratulatory message on the 25th anniversary of Ikeda's first visit to the Soviet Union (*Seikyo Shimbun*, September 8, 1999).

Nichiren. 1999. *The Writings of Nichiren Daishonin.* Tokyo: Soka Gakkai.

Ruff, Tillman. "The Health and Environmental Effects of Nuclear Weapons" in *SGI Quarterly*, October 2010.

SGI Quarterly. 2005. "Bodhisattva Never Disparaging: The Path of Respect." Retrieved on July 24, 2012 from <http://www.sgiquarterly.org/buddhism2005Apr-1.html>.

Schell, Jonathan. 1982. *The Fate of the Earth.* New York: Knopf.

Tannenwald, Nina. 2007. *The Nuclear Taboo: The United States and the Non-use of Nuclear Weapons since 1945.* Cambridge: Cambridge University Press.

The Weapons of Mass Destruction Commission. 2006. *Weapons of Terror: Freeing the World of Nuclear, Biological and Chemical Arms* (June 2006).

Toda, Josei. 1957. "Declaration Calling for the Abolition of Nuclear Weapons" (September 8, 1957, Yokohama). Retrieved on July 24, 2012 from <http://www.joseitoda.org/vision/declaration/read>.

Weeramantry, Christopher. 1996. Dissenting Opinion on "Legality of the Threat or Use of Nuclear Weapons" – International Court of Justice Advisory Opinion of 8 July 1996 (General List No. 95, 1995–98).

Index

DAISAKU IKEDA AND DIALOGUE FOR PEACE

Toda Institute for Global Peace and Policy
    Research xviii, xxi, xxii, 1, 3, 127
Toda, Josei 7, 59, 84, 117, 125, 126
    and Buddha 17
    influence of xiii, xiv, xxii
    and nuclear weapons 145, 146
Todd, Sharon 44–5
Togo 123
Tokyo conference 3
Tokyo Fuji Art Museum xviii, 126–27
Toynbee, Arnold xxiii, 6, 8, 22, 30, 46, 99
    and Buddhism 23–5
    and human history 2, 63
Treaty on the Non-Proliferation of Nuclear
    Weapons (NPT) 151
Tropin, Vladimir Ivanovich 27–8
Troyanovsky, Alexander 26
trust 15, 126, 132
Tu Weiming 43, 84, 91–2, 99
Twenty Years of Encounters (Tropin) 28
Twitter 66
two truths 49

"Uniqueness and Recurrence in History"
    (Toynbee) 8
United Nations xix, xx, 14, 83, 123
    and China 25
    and dialogue xxii
    and nuclear weapons 151, 152
United Nations Mission in Sierra Leone
    (UNAMSIL) 123
United States of America (USA) xvii, 2,
    6, 25
    and China 26
    and education xviii, 97
    and Ikeda 30–1
    and nuclear weapons 146
    and the Soviet Union xix
universe, the 16–17, 53
unrest 129
Urbain, Olivier 39, 41
    and conflict 45–6
    and dialogue 62–3, 64
    and humanitarian competition 42

USSR *see* Soviet Union

violence 2, 13, 14, 74, 77, 86, 117
    and education 94–5, 97
    and globalization xxi
    and Japan xviii
    and nuclear weapons 143, 149, 153
    and racism 72
    see also nonviolence

Waldheim, Kurt 30
war 13, 14, 30, 89, 117, 120
    and nuclear weapons 141–42, 143
Weeramantry, Christopher 142
Weil, Simone xxii–xxiii
Whitman, Walt xvii
Wider, Sarah 39–40
Wikileaks xvii
Wilson, Bryan 99, 100
wisdom xviii, 126
women's rights 75
world history 103–5
World Is Yours to Change, The 40–1
World of Yesterday, The (Zweig) xxii
world peace xiv, xv, 1–2, 28
World War II xix, xxii, 89

xenophobia xxii

Yalman, Nur 3, 43, 100
Yamamoto, Hideo 29–30
young people 62, 67–8
    and bullying 97
    and discussion meetings 70–1
    and nuclear weapons 152
    and peace 92
    and social networking 66–7, 68
    see also children; Muslim youth

Zhou Enlai 6, 22, 26, 29, 144
Zoroastrianism 111
Zweig, Stefan xxii